RETROSPECTIVES FOR EVERYONE

POWERFUL METAPHORS FOR EFFECTIVE RETROSPECTIVES

MADHAVI LEDALLA

INDIA • SINGAPORE • MALAYSIA

Notion Press

No. 8, 3rd Cross Street
CIT Colony, Mylapore
Chennai, Tamil Nadu – 600004

First Published by Notion Press 2020
Copyright © Madhavi Ledalla 2020
All Rights Reserved.

ISBN 978-1-64760-849-1

This book has been published with all efforts taken to make the material error-free after the consent of the author. However, the author and the publisher do not assume and hereby disclaim any liability to any party for any loss, damage, or disruption caused by errors or omissions, whether such errors or omissions result from negligence, accident, or any other cause.

While every effort has been made to avoid any mistake or omission, this publication is being sold on the condition and understanding that neither the author nor the publishers or printers would be liable in any manner to any person by reason of any mistake or omission in this publication or for any action taken or omitted to be taken or advice rendered or accepted on the basis of this work. For any defect in printing or binding the publishers will be liable only to replace the defective copy by another copy of this work then available.

Dedication

To Mom and Dad, who saw potential in my creativity and without questioning it's meaning encouraged me to join classes to explore my expressions. This was the starting point of my journey of using creations in my work.
To my husband and daughters for being my pillars of strength.
To my Agile community as my partners in this journey.

CONTENTS

Foreword – Diana Larsen *11*
Foreword – Luke Hohmann *15*
Preface *17*
Acknowledgements *19*
Recommendations *21*
Who must Read This Book? *23*
How to Read This Book? *25*

Chapter 1: Introduction **27**
1. Agile Frameworks 28
2. Agile Team 31
3. Beyond IT 32
4. Retrospectives for Everyone 33
5. Retrospectives Overview 35
6. Backstage of Retrospectives 37
7. Getting Started 38
8. Retrospective Course – the Essential Rs. 40
9. Advantages 42

Chapter 2: Situation Specific Collaboration Frameworks **45**
1. Logistics and Room Setup 46
2. Materials 47

Chapter 3: Framework Clusters **49**

PART 1: NURTURE TEAM WORK

Chapter 4: Nurture Teamwork **53**
1. Shoot the Ball 55
2. Journey. 58
3. Highway Drive. 59
4. Fly High. 61
5. Team Values 63
6. Rowing a Boat 65
7. Remote Control 67
8. Blind Men and the Elephant 69
9. Tandem Bicycle 71

PART 2: MANAGE CHANGE

Chapter 5: Manage Change. **75**
1. Snakes and Ladders 77
2. Holistic View 79
3. Vicious Cycle 81
4. Chilly Autumn. 83
5. Candle Flame. 85
6. Scuba Diving 87
7. Complacent Rabbit 89

PART 3: PRODUCT LEADERSHIP

Chapter 6: Product Leadership **93**
1. Garden Your Thoughts. 95
2. Magic Lamp. 97
3. Dream Product. 99
4. Nurture the Plant. 101
5. Product Eel 103
6. Mushroom Cloud 105
7. Time Travel 107

PART 4: OBJECTIVE FOCUSED

Chapter 7: Objective-focused **111**
1. The Bottleneck... 112
2. Climbing a Mountain 114
3. Spotlight 116
4. Retro Clock 118
5. Bow and Arrow 120
6. Rapid Fire 122
7. Perfect Day.. 123
8. Speed Up 125

PART 5: CONTINOUS REFLECTION

Chapter 8: Continuous Reflection **129**
1. Right Forecast 130
2. Value Delivery 132
3. Milestones Map 134
4. Data Center 136
5. An Avoidable Fire... 143
6. Impediments Map 145
7. Dependencies Map... 146
8. Retro Radiator 147

PART 6: GOING BEYOND THE ROUTINE

Chapter 9: Going Beyond the Routine **151**
1. Team Yaan 152
2. Set Me Free 154
3. Up Cycle 156
4. Foresee the Future 158
5. Delay Cost Balloon 159
6. Tasty Cake 161

PART 7: PERSONAL REFLECTION

Chapter 10: Personal Reflection 167
1. Three Monkeys 168
2. The Best "you" 170
3. Value tree 172
4. Model Your Sprint 174
5. Picture Your Sprint 175
6. The Chemical Reaction 177

PART 8: ADDRESS THE STATE OF MIND

Chapter 11: Address the State of Mind 181
1. Pulse Check 183
2. The Balance 185
3. Safe Space 187
4. Positive Sandbox 189
5. Roundtable 192
6. Dream Catcher 194
7. Balanced Sandbox 196

PART 9: ADDING LAYERS TO RETROSPECTIVES

Chapter 12: Adding Layers to Retrospectives 201
1. Daily Retrospectives 202
2. Cross-team Retrospectives 204
3. Distributed Retrospectives 209
4. Release Retrospectives 213
5. Leveraging Online Collaboration Tools 219
6. Using a Combination of Collaboration Frameworks 220
7. Using the Same Technique in Different Contexts 223

PART 10: TIPS AND TRICKS

Chapter 13: Tips and Tricks **227**
1. Effective Retrospectives Checklist. 228
2. Retrospectives Health Radar. 231
3. Retrospective Anti Patterns. 235
4. Retrospective Maturity Levels. 238
5. Retrospective Feedback. 239
6. Embrace the Real World. 241

Epilogue *245*
About the Author. *247*

FOREWORD - DIANA LARSEN

I first met Madhavi Ledalla at the Agile India conference in 2015. Her passion for effective retrospectives infused our conversation, and I was drawn in. At that meeting, she shared her first few metaphors with me (and with the conference in a workshop). Madhavi impressed me with her facility for combining retrospectives with visualizing work and creating a powerful fusion for team learning.

In 2006, Esther Derby and I wrote and published, *"Agile Retrospectives: Making Good Teams Great"*, the first book to describe an iterative continuous learning and improvement group process for software teams. For years before that publication, we met annually with a group of colleagues in the Retrospective Facilitators Gathering (RFG) events to build on and extend Norman L. Kerth's ideas about end-of-project retrospectives to fit the incremental delivery nature of agile software development approaches. The focus on team autonomy in the work as well as continuous feedback, learning and improvement were foundations of the practice.

Beginning in 2013, with the publication of Patrick Kua's "*The Retrospective Handbook: A guide for teams*", new books began to appear to enlarge on the ideas Esther and I had proposed. Now a quick search on amazon.com for retrospectives results in a list of eight books on the topic. If you add a search for similar processes, you'll find additional books like Jesper Boes' "*Level Up with Toyota Kata*", website resources like https://retromat.org curated by Corinna Baldauf, and much more retrospectives have gone world-wide in a relatively short period of time. Sticky notes for collocated teams and virtual tools for retros with remote teams abound!

When teams hold effective retros, they gain real improvement in their teamwork, work processes, output quality and professional skills. With all the resources available you might expect that all teams everywhere would be exhibiting amazing results. Unfortunately, on the cusp of 2020, more teams treat retrospectives as a box to check on their project management forms and get through it as quickly as possible, rather than as a useful, valuable opportunity for learning. Clearly, a new perspective can add to that potential. New readers need new expressions.

Since that meeting with Madhavi in India, we have stayed in contact as she has enhanced and amplified her ideas. Through the years she has shared her progress and that progress has culminated in "*Retrospectives for Everyone*". In it, she extends the use of the retrospective group process beyond software teams. As the title asserts, retrospectives ARE for everyone!

In the pages of this book, you'll find a refreshing and intriguing approach to the work of reflection, learning, and improvement. As Ms. Ledalla tells us here, any team, group, community, organization, or (dare I say?) family, can find a metaphor to fit their situation. Her emphasis on reflection sets a tone for learning and improvement suitable for many challenges faced by human systems. Even when that system is a single individual learner as in the group of frameworks for Personal Reflection.

One more thing: Whether you are an experienced artist, graphic recorder, sketch noter, or someone who doesn't think they can draw a straight line, you will find rich inspiration in the example illustrations of these metaphors.

Welcome to this wealth of new ways to think about, design, and enliven your retrospective meetings! I hope you enjoy reading and applying its metaphors as much as I have.

Onward!
Diana Larsen
Co-author, *"Agile Retrospectives: Making Good Teams Great"*
Co-founder & Chief Connector, Agile Fluency Project (AFP) LLC

* * *

BIOGRAPHY

A visionary pragmatist, Diana Larsen is Chief Connector and co-founder at the Agile Fluency® Project LLC. We hold an exciting vision for the future: "Every agile software team practices Software Development at a level of fluent proficiency that specifically fits their businesses' needs." During her extensive career, Diana has worked with business leaders to design work systems, improve project performance, inspire teams to greatness, and support leader and enterprise agility. Now, she prepares the ground for other agile leaders to achieve similar results, building on the foundation of the Agile Fluency Suite.

Currently, in her spare time, she delivers inspiring conference keynote talks, facilitates productive Open Space Technology events, and enjoys time with her grandchildren, friends, and family.

FOREWORD - LUKE HOHMANN

Retrospectives are arguably the single most important practice in agile, but only if one acts on the results and that requires more than a meeting. As a community, we've known this for, quite literally, decades.

And yet, far too often, we continue to see organizations fail to gain the power of retrospectives for any number of reasons:

- They fail to properly plan for the retrospective. And without a plan, the retrospective fails to create actionable insights
- They fail to act on the insights generated by the retrospective
- They fail to tailor the retrospective technique to match the needs of the team
- They fail to include remote or distributed teams in the process
- They fail to focus on the individual, the team and the organization.

With so many ways to fail, we need a guide to help us succeed.

In this insightful and personal book, Madhavi Ledalla gives us all a guide that can help us improve our retrospectives. And though there are many good books on available retrospectives, this book is a unique contribution, replete with fresh insights and techniques.

Read it. Use it. Share it.

Luke Hohmann
Founder and CEO of Conteneo
Author of the book- "Innovation Games®"

* * *

BIOGRAPHY

Luke Hohmann is the Founder and CEO of Conteneo (previously known as The Innovation Games® Company; https://conteneo.co/). The author of three books, Luke's playfully diverse background of life experiences has uniquely prepared him to design and produce serious games. Luke graduated magna cum laude with a BSE in computer engineering and an MSE in computer science and engineering from the University of Michigan. He is also a former National Junior Pairs Figure Skating Champion as well as a certified aerobics instructor. In his spare time, Luke likes roughhousing with his four kids and his wife's cooking. Luke's a bit of an old school Silicon Valley entrepreneur. Instead of building a company to flip, he's building a company to change the world. You can join him by playing games at Weave (https://weave.scaledagile.com/) or Every Voice Engaged (https://www.everyvoiceengaged.org/).

PREFACE

I am Madhavi Ledalla, based on Marcus Buckingham's personality assessment, my personality type is CREATOR|TEACHER. I have experience in traditional and agile methodologies. When I started using agile methodology, I went through the ups and downs of a typical agile team. While working as a Scrum Master, I was overwhelmed with the amount of value this role carries and it motivated me to choose agile coaching as a career path. My role as a coach allowed me to work with a broader spectrum where I could interact and learn from all layers in the organization.

As I was responsible to coach teams towards becoming self-organized, my aim was to serve them and enable them to operate at their highest potential. In the process, make myself redundant so that teams could function by themselves. This is where I started researching and finding ways to facilitate team conversations using situational specific methods.

I was figuring out ways to make team discussions engaging and resourceful. My approach was to get a sense of the situation and experiment with techniques for facilitating team conversations that would allow them to reflect and come up with ideas and thoughts by themselves.

During one of my coaching engagements, I got an opportunity to work with Luke Hohmann, where I have used Sail Boat[1] Innovation game to facilitate a large distributed team retrospective for the whole organization. This allowed me to appreciate the impact of visual collaboration frameworks, and this awareness inspired me to continue to leverage and research around this concept.

[1.] https://retrospectivewiki.org/index.php?title=Sailboat

I also used the concepts from the book - "*Agile Retrospectives: Making Good Teams Great*"[2] by Esther Derby and Diana Larsen. This is a great resource when it comes to learning core concepts about retrospectives and would definitely help in appreciating how retrospectives are incredibly valuable to any team.

While using such creative avenues of visualization, I noticed an improvement in team engagement levels and it encouraged me to continue exploring and gain deeper insights into creating situational specific methods for facilitating team dialogues.

I could relate real time scenarios that I was seeing around me for a few of the team contexts. So, this flashed the idea to try and see how I could make use of these real-world instances for mirroring reflections. This is when I tried using metaphors like Kite Flying, Mangal Yaan, Mountain Climbing as frameworks for collaboration and I could see a positive transformation in the interactions. These illustrations were helpful in creating an environment where teams could relate to it naturally and thus aided in fruitful insights coming out.

I also got to work with various industries and conducted training across departments that included HR, operations, marketing and sales. I was surprised to see how these teams were able to relate to concepts to think through their current situations and come up with alternatives and explore possibilities.

The facilitator plays a crucial part in implementing these frameworks. Those who are passionate about creating an environment to foster lively discussions, and who believe in the power of visualization and who value team involvement would be able to appreciate and relate to these approaches.

Since 2013, I started creating these frameworks and I blogged about them and received positive feedback from professionals around the globe on how they were able to use the same. This feedback encouraged me to continue my exploration and I posted some of these techniques on Scrum Alliance and Agile Connection. I believe I learned more by sharing and hence thought of collating all my ideas, and experiments at one place in this book so that readers can locate them with ease. I look forward to receiving feedback from all of you.

[2.] https://www.amazon.in/Agile-Retrospectives-Making-Pragmatic-Programmers/dp/0977616649

ACKNOWLEDGEMENTS

This book would not have been possible without the constant support provided by my family, friends, mentors, colleagues and my agile community. Writing a book was much more difficult than I thought and more rewarding than I could have ever imagined. I am eternally grateful to the ecosystem I am surrounded by, for standing by me throughout.

Journaling about the journey of how I have used my experiences and reflections at work was possible because of my professional network. I would like to thank them for being open to my ideas and allowing me to experiment. I'm forever indebted to all the organizations and my teams for their ongoing support. It is because of their motivation that I have a legacy to pass on to my agile community.

My agile journey started with Intergraph Private Limited. The support extended by the teams and leadership has added great value in my learning progression and project management journey.

SolutionsIQ was another major milestone in my agile career. I am grateful to them for offering me to consult with various organizations as an agile coach. Thanks to all the coaches at SolutionsIQ and Vibhu Srinivasan for giving me the opportunity to be part of this wonderful learning platform. Special thanks to my colleagues Antara Pal Chaudhary and Arun Jayaraman for partnering with me during my conference presentations.

In my current role at ADP, I am thankful to the entire leadership group, coaches and all my teams for giving me the opportunity to work with them. I feel elated to be part of a product-oriented organization that promotes creativity and encourages employees to grow.

Thank you, Brent Barton, Luke Hohmann and Diana Larsen, for being my constant source of inspiration for writing this book. I am grateful to have mentors like you in my life. I would also like to thank Vikas Uppal, a friend of mine in the virtual collaboration space for the feedback and inputs. Thank you Micheal Delamaza for reviewing my book and giving me inputs on the assessment framework for retrospectives. I would also like to express my gratitude to Jutta Ekinsten for the thorough review of the entire book.

My agile community associates and guides Cherie Silas, Arne Ahlander, Steve Spearman, Sabine Canditt, Daniel Gullo, Jeff Lopez, Vernon Stinebeker, Kamal Manglani and Nanda Lankalapalli, I thank them for having my back throughout my journey. Also, I am glad to meet and learn from Naveen Najundappa, Jayaprakash Puttaswamy, Jaya Srivatsava, Sekhar Burra, Vijay Bandaru, PV Anantha Ramaiah, Saket Bansal, Rajshekhar Chittoory and Narasimha Reddy Bommaka. Thanks to my agile friends Soma Bhattacharya, Sairam Chamarthi, Sathish Chandrasekaran, Vivek Ganesan and Purav Shah for the lively discussions.

Special thanks to my cousin Shreya Banda who believed in the idea behind the book and worked passionately to enhance the manuscripts tone and voice. Thanks to my cousins Divya Banda Pogaru and Sindhu Kamaraju for their encouragement.

I am grateful to the organizers and chairs of Agile India, Discuss Agile, Agile Hyderabad, Lean Kanban, India Scrum Enthusiasts Community (ISEC) and Scrum Alliance conferences, for giving me the opportunity to share my work.

Special thanks to Sir Soma Sekhar for helping me with the creatives for this book.

Finally, to everyone who has been with me in this journey; by attending my talks at conferences, reading and liking my blogs - thank you for being the inspiration and foundation for my project management and coaching journey.

RECOMMENDATIONS

Retrospective is the core of any agile learning for an agile team. Madhavi captures these set of practices uniquely designed to accelerate a team's learning process. A must read for agile teams!

– **Kamal Manglani**, *Former Agile Lead eBay,
Co-Author of Product Takeoff*

Teams are different and the things that they have to deal with can differ from sprint to sprint; having a "toolbox of exercises" helps you as a retrospective facilitator to better serve your teams. The frameworks in this book provide you with lots of different ways to do agile retrospectives. Try them out, experiment and learn to ensure that your retrospectives truly help teams to improve themselves!

– **Ben Linders**,
Author of the book – "Getting Value out of Agile Retrospectives"

This book is really a great advice with a very concrete example on how the different metaphors have been used by the author. It inspires to use the metaphors as they are, adapt them and to create our own

– **Jutta Eckstein**, *Author, Coach,
Consultant and Trainer*

I have known Madhavi Ledalla for several years. She has always been enthusiastic about running retrospectives passionately. She used to come up with various metaphors for different situations. This approach really connects the participants with their situation well and retrospectives would be more effective. This book is a compilation of all her hard work over the years. She has excellent creative skills that helped us come up with the right picture for the metaphor she wants to use.

– *Nanda Lankalapalli CST*,
ACC (ICF)

I have been using some of the techniques cited in this book with my teams that include Team Journey, Fly High and Team Yaan. I feel though these frameworks are different analogies of the simple retrospective techniques, they channelize the team to think beyond the three basics (what went well, what didn't go well and what more to improve). Some of the usual concerns that I was able to overcome by using these techniques are: team is not motivated to attend, team usually requests to skip the retrospective or not able to capture every member's thought process in the retrospective and many others.

– *Hasanti Chavali*,
Project Manager, ADP

Retrospectives are extremely valuable activities that aren't given the right level of importance. At the same time, the traditional way to conduct them allows for serious dysfunctions and little value-add. This book crosses those chasms. Collaboration-frameworks based retrospectives are effective and fun. This collection of retrospectives, many of them created by Ledalla, are a great source for myriad needs.

– *Masa K. Maeda*,
PhD. CEO of Valueinnova LLC USA.,
Founder and Principal Consultant

WHO MUST READ THIS BOOK?

This book can be used by individuals for personal reflection and by teams as well. The techniques presented here are intended to give you a toolkit of approaches that can be useful during team discussions, which will be helpful in exploring unknowns and thus can help facilitate tough conversations.

This book does not get into details of agile and Scrum frameworks as readers are assumed to have knowledge about these. In case anyone would like to review the Scrum guide to get a deeper understanding of the framework, then here is the resource for the guide[3].

[3.] https://www.scrumguides.org/

HOW TO READ THIS BOOK?

This book is divided into chapters that initially introduce the concept of agile, retrospectives, describes different collaboration frameworks and then guides the reader to come up with their own frameworks for facilitation.

The book starts with familiarizing the concept of agile, the different agile frameworks and then discusses how agile, and retrospectives can be universally applied to any industry. The concept of collaboration frameworks is then introduced and the framework clusters are described.

- The first part of the book introduces frameworks that can be used to nurture team collaboration and help in team bonding.
- The second part of the book introduces frameworks that can be used to deal with change and how it can be effectively handled as a norm rather than an exception.
- The third part throws light on the frameworks that can be used by Product leaders for visioning, road mapping and prioritizing.
- The fourth part of the book discusses frameworks that can be used to help strategize and follow up on goals and plans.
- The fifth part of the book shows you ways to ensure a continuous reflection rather than one-time reflections at regular intervals.
- The sixth part describes how the creative potential can be leveraged for reflections.
- The seventh part puts forth ideas for personal retrospection and analysis.

➤ The eighth part of the book talks about frameworks that can be applied to dwell upon one's state of mind for self-reflection.

➤ The chapter that follows touches upon how reflections in a multi-team, release and distributed setups can be eased.

➤ The last chapter summarizes some pointers around an effective engagement, evaluating the retrospective health and finally the most important piece talks about how the real-world situations can be leveraged to create meaningful reflections.

It may happen that sometimes the approaches cited in this book may not be appropriate to your team situation and frameworks described may not seem to be relevant during your first try. My recommendation to you is that - keep experimenting and see how it works. This will help you learn as you implement and give you room to inspect and adapt, and create something new for your team needs if required. Believe me, once you appreciate the unique flavor that these types of collaboration frameworks bring to the table, you cannot stop yourself from inventing new ones!

INTRODUCTION

CHAPTER **01**

According to the agile manifesto, agile shares a unique perspective of working with people that allows one to be nimble, embrace change, move swiftly and be responsive to changing market conditions and customer expectations. Agile values and principles talk about guidelines that focus on a collaborative culture and customer centricity to deliver the highest business value. The heartbeat of agile are happy and engaged teams that make things happen. Agile practices recommend teams to take ownership and be accountable for their work.

I am sure all of us appreciate why we need to respond to change, why change is inevitable and why we need to collaborate with customers. If we reflect on the agile manifesto[4], we see that the approach and philosophy of agile enables us to do these.

The agile philosophy, which values teamwork, change management, collaboration, and working in small increments are applicable to any industry well beyond product and engineering teams. Agile was initially limited to a few software engineering teams, however progressively it has become a norm and the popularity of its philosophy has made organizations from various sectors adapt its principles. The State of Agile[5] report stands evidence to this change, and everyone is moving to being agile to keep pace with the volatile market needs and demands.

***

[4.] https://agilemanifesto.org/
[5.] https://www.stateofagile.com/

1. AGILE FRAMEWORKS

Agile software development is a group of software development methodologies based on iterative and incremental development. It is an umbrella term for a set of frameworks and practices based on the values and principles expressed in the manifesto for agile software development. Scrum, DSDM, Crystal, XP and FDD are examples of agile frameworks, which emphasize philosophies of continuous planning, empowered teams, collaboration and emergent design.

Scrum, developed by a group of renowned developers that included Ken Schwaber, Jeff Sutherland and Mike Beedle, is an empirical framework for developing and sustaining complex products. It comprises certain best practices, roles, events and artifacts. Scrum concentrates on the management aspects of software development, dividing development into one to four-week sprints. Scrum places less emphasis on engineering practices and many teams combine Scrum with extreme programming practices for achieving engineering excellence.

Extreme programming (XP) developed by Kent Beck is a software development methodology which is intended to improve software quality and responsiveness to the changing customer requirements. It is a framework which focuses on continuously improving the quality of the delivered product through some core practices that include Test Driven Development, Continuous Integration, Automation, Small Releases and Pair Programming.

Dynamic Systems Development Method (DSDM) is one of the agile methods for developing software and it forms part of the Agile Alliance. DSDM focuses on Information Systems projects that are characterized by tight schedules and budgets. It's coverage of the project lifecycle is broad from feasibility and business case to implementation.

Crystal developed by Alistair Cockburn is a family of methodologies designed for projects ranging from those run by small teams developing low criticality systems to those run by large teams building high criticality systems. The crystal framework provides a great example of how we can tailor a method to match the characteristics of a project and an organization.

Feature-Driven Development (FDD) developed by Jeff De Luca is a simple-to-understand yet powerful approach to build products or solutions. A project team following the FDD method will first develop an overall model for the product, build a feature list and plan the work. The team then moves through the design and builds sprints to develop the features.

Depending on the context of the scenario and certain key information regarding the need, one needs to choose a framework. Let us consider this statement with an example.

You need to create a request for a painting for a marketing project. Assume that this need has the following constraints:

a. Time

b. Budget allocated

c. Adaptability

d. Target market

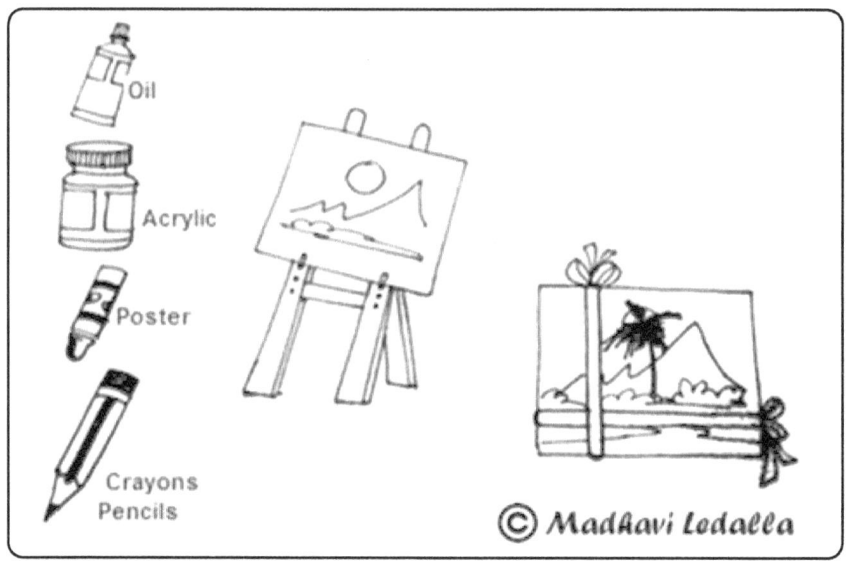

There could be many other constraints depending on the nature of the organization and product.

The choice of paint is left to the discretion of the artist. Oil paints give it the classic impact, water colors offer a casual touch, pencil sketching gets points for creative effect and poster colors are easily adaptable.

It is worth remembering the old adage "one size does not fit all". Similarly, you can use multiple frameworks to achieve agility. But the selection of the framework depends on the constraints involved. The aim is to satisfy the maximum number of constraints which would facilitate the desired outcome.

For example, Scrum can be used in an empirical environment that relies on frequent inspection and adaptation. Here things can be planned for the specific duration of the sprint, for the next incremental change. For example, Kanban developed by Taiichi Ohno uses a set of principles and practices that can be used in any business function be it sales, marketing, software development or operations for managing and improving the flow of work and which in turn improves the underlying process. Therefore, the choice of the framework depends on the context and the nature of the problem domain.

Agile values and principles help achieve the most valuable outcomes in the shortest time frame – these concepts could be used at work or in life. They apply to any industry where the focus is on the right kind of outcome. The techniques mentioned in this book could also be used by any function like human resources, finance, IT, sales or marketing, and I will also extend it by saying you could use these techniques in schools and colleges as well to work with students.

* * *

2. AGILE TEAM

The team is the core element in agile – they work for a common objective. A distinguishing feature from other teams is that the agile team does not have a hierarchy. This means that regardless of the individual work, accountability rests with the entire team.

In the agile manifesto the first proclaimed value is to prioritize "individuals and interactions over processes and tools". The success of an agile team is inherently linked to the characteristics of its members and their relationships. Getting the right people to the right roles in agile teams is therefore critical for an accomplished journey of the team, as they are expected to be self-organizing and cross-functional.

Team collaboration is a key driving factor for agile teams. It is all about their interactions and their collaborative spirit to aim at their shared purpose. Self-organizing means the team should be able to plan, execute and come up with the best possible solutions to deliver their work. They are told what the work is and they take complete ownership regarding how to do the work. Cross functionality refers to the fact that agile teams consist of people from all departments and functions required to deliver the work end-to-end. This may include but is not limited to IT, sales, marketing, HR and operations.

* * *

3. BEYOND IT

Agile can be used by any team that anticipates changes and needs to make course corrections based on their customer or stakeholder feedback. Agile enables teams to deliver value faster with greater quality and predictability, with an ability to embrace and respond to change. Value can be variable depending on what kind of team you belong to. The value is the increment that the teams produce at the end of every time-boxed duration.

The definition of increment depends on the context of the industry. For IT industries, the increment could be a piece of working functionality, for non-IT industries this piece could be anything that adds value. For HR, this could be the number of potential hires or the number of shortlisted candidates. For a sales team, it could mean the number of sales that they closed. For an operations team, it could be the number of tickets closed. For marketing, it could be campaign roll outs and tracking its outcome. Whereas, for research teams, it could be about the research and its findings. Agile is quickly becoming the preferred way to manage projects in businesses. Irrespective of their domain of work, organizations today, are looking for a cutting edge and flexible system that keeps them competitive and responsive. Agile has moved beyond IT companies and teams.

* * *

4. RETROSPECTIVES FOR EVERYONE

"Learn from yesterday, live for today, hope for tomorrow. The important thing is not to stop questioning." – Albert Einstein

Retrospectives are platforms for teams and individuals to look back and reflect on positives, at the same time look at areas that need a different outlook which will help them improve their journey ahead.

Change is disruptive and one cannot run away from it. Agile welcomes change and encourages teams to be flexible and adaptable. If teams have to work at a sustained pace in this fast-changing environment, then there needs to be a platform where teams can continuously reflect and adapt. Retrospectives provide platforms for teams to do this at a continuum.

Retrospectives are all about reflection and thinking about lessons of the past to get better in the future. Teams need to constantly ponder on ways to improve in order to aim higher. This applies to everyone's personal lives as well, where we continuously opine on our journey, where we want to go next and what we can do differently.

Reflecting on the past around diversified areas like work-life balance, goals, team collaboration, product development, process, technology, delivery or targets is an ongoing process that happens either explicitly or implicitly. It can be on the personal, professional and industrial fronts, and hence this concept is universally applicable to everyone, for reflecting on the past and envisioning a better tomorrow.

Retrospection can also happen on a day-to-day basis or over a period of a time box. This time box could be a week, a month or even one year. The retrospection can be focused around a specific issue or it can be generic. While retrospection is constant, the format and motivations could differ. The frameworks could be customized and used depending on the context and through this book you will learn about different ways for facilitating retrospectives.

* * *

5. RETROSPECTIVES OVERVIEW

"Stop being afraid of what could go wrong, and start being excited of what could go right". – *Tony Robbins*

Retrospectives are the primary learning, reflection and readjustment techniques specifically aimed at the "inspect and adapt" behavior of a team. In Scrum, retrospectives are one of the events that take place after every sprint during which team members gather to inspect how the sprint went and identify areas for improvements. Retrospectives help teams to assess their strengths and weaknesses and come up with some strategies to become stronger.

Here is how I visualize the essence of effective retrospectives:

R -> Reflect on where you are and where you want to be
E -> Engage the teams in fruitful discussions
T -> Team work to build "We over I" attitude
R -> Realize the power of Inspect and Adapt cycles
O -> Openness among the team builds a trusted relationship
S -> Share your pain and pleasure points openly
P -> Platform to celebrate success and ponder upon failures
E -> Eliminate activities that do not add value during the journey
C -> Courage to speak the right things and work on tough problems
T -> Transparency among team members makes retrospectives efficient and effective
I –> Inspect on process improvements
V -> Vibrant with discussions around the current state and happenings
E -> Engrossed in coming up with actionable conclusions at the end of the retrospective so that team has a solid take away

I view retrospectives as an opportunity to coach team members. Let us take a slight step away from retrospectives to understand the **GROUP** coaching model, which is a powerful coaching model.

- **Goal** - Determines the focus of coaching
- **Reality** - Raises awareness of present realities and examines how the current situation is impacting the group's goals

- **Options** - While identifying and assessing available options, encourages solution focused thinking and brainstorming

- **Understanding** - Group observes and notices their internal responses to what is being said and creates meaning of what they hear and their internal response. The group connects to the emerging best future

- **Perform** - Assists the group to determine next steps, prototype best options and develop individual and group action plans

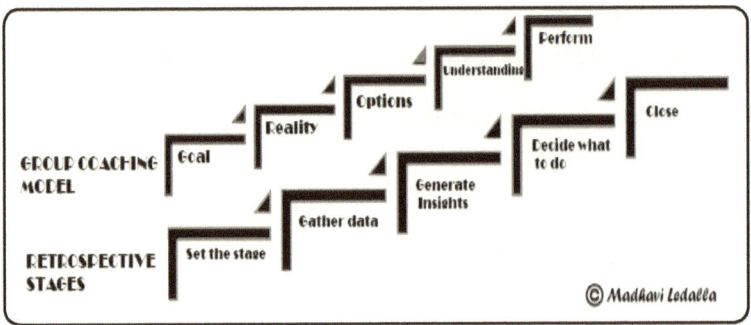

This GROUP coaching model is comparable to the five stages of a retrospective - Set the stage, Gather Data, Generate Insights and Create Action Items, and Close the retrospective as mentioned by Esther Derby and Diana Larsen in their book "Agile Retrospectives"[6].

* * *

[6.] https://www.amazon.in/Agile-Retrospectives-Making-Pragmatic-Programmers/dp/0977616649

6. BACKSTAGE OF RETROSPECTIVES

A retrospective is not any new concept or jargon that the team needs to master - but yes, in reality it becomes challenging to keep the momentum lively at all times in a few cases! After a couple of retrospectives, teams start complaining about losing interest in the retrospective and its effectiveness is lost.

There could be many reasons for such situations to arise and an ineffective retrospective can transform into something like mentioned below:

R -> Repeated issues pop-up
E -> Engrossing discussions are missing
T -> Team members are present virtually and not involved
R -> Routine stuff, nothing interests teams
O -> Observably gets boring over time
S -> Spectators break the trusted and open culture
P -> Problems during the sprint are not discussed openly
E -> Engaging discussions are missing
C -> Constructive feedback becomes argumentative
T -> Trust is lost among team members
I -> Intimacy between team members is lacking
V -> Vague action items without any outcome
E -> Ends up as a blame game

This triggers a need to do something differently and break the usual norms, so that these retrospectives could be made thought-provoking exercises. Also, maybe one can think differently based on the teams' journey so far and try different variations for the meetings to help the team think out-of-the-box, discover options and explore them.

This book highlights the importance of retrospectives and then goes through some of the common challenges and puts forth a few thoughts on how to make them thought-provoking.

The frameworks presented in the book can be used for individuals and teams. Some of them are very specific to a few focus areas, you will understand as you read this book. This book has been divided into different chapters based on the techniques and the applicability for different focus groups.

* * *

7. GETTING STARTED

While retrospectives could be used by anyone, a few simple steps that can help you get started are described below.

Team:

- **Identify the team:** i.e., the group of people who are working towards a shared purpose
- **Identify the focus for the team:** Understand why the team is brought together, what are the expectations and what are they supposed to achieve or work towards
- **Identify the current state:** Try to get the pulse of how the team is working, how their journey has been so far, what is working well for them, what are they struggling with and what are their future aspirations, if any
- **Identify the team context:** Try to spot the area where you think the team can improve or can debate on a better way of working. See where you can help the team by helping them mirror themselves using any of the frameworks cited in this book
- **Identify a framework:** Select a relevant collaboration idea that can help the team feel closer to their context and thus can relate to it and brainstorm on hypotheses and realities
- **Identify a cadence:** Encourage teams to continue the rhythm for reflection without breaks for sustainable visible improvements and reflections.

Personal:

For personal reflections the method is pretty much similar as mentioned above for teams. Here are some pointers that may help:

- Reflect where you are, what your aspirations are and how your personal journey has been
- Think about the barriers that you came across during your journey
- Figure out which one is bothering you most

▶ Pick any framework that can help you visualize the journey so far, and try to think in terms of things that helped and hindered your journey, and start from there

▶ Remember these frameworks will not give you any solutions to your problems, they just enable you to visualize yourself in a mirror

The power of visualization is that when you spot the problem and can actually see it, the solution organically emerges in most cases as you know what the issue is. Visualization helps you come up with a clean state of mind with reduced stress levels and thus you can now paint a picture of yourself in terms of very subjective evidence from your past and aspirations into your future. These frameworks indirectly help you become more mindful about your ambitions, so you can visualize your personal self and thus guide you on the next steps.

※ ※ ※

8. RETROSPECTIVE COURSE – THE ESSENTIAL RS.

Here are some pointers that can help a team organize its retrospectives course. These perspectives are based on the basic five stages of a retrospective as mentioned by Esther Derby and Diana Larsen, in their book *"Agile Retrospectives- Making Good Teams Great"* [7].

1. **Reflection on the need for a retrospective:** Greet team members and explain the purpose of the retrospective. Introduce the prime directive of the retrospective as explained by Norm Kerth[8] in the book *"Project Retrospectives"* - Regardless of what we discover, the team truly understands and believes that everyone did the best job they could, given what they knew at the time, their skills, their abilities, the resources available and the situation on hand.

    Reinforce that the retrospective is meant for the team to gather feedback and discuss from different perspectives that include people, processes and tools, and technology. Discuss ground rules related to what conversation is acceptable (free conversation about the problem areas) and what is not (individual criticism). Reiterate that the purpose is to share insights and learn from each other and not to blame or call out on personal issues. This level setting is important to encourage open and honest communication.

    The main aim of this step is to explain the purpose and to create a safe environment for people to start conversing.

2. **Reflection on the current:** In this step a shared vision of what happened in the time-boxed period of reflection is created. The team can discuss on what was going well, what wasn't, what impediments they faced, what they have learned over a period of time and what they would do differently in the future. This step requires intense brainstorming and reflection on the time-boxed duration so that there is enough data to discuss and debate, and here is where the facilitation using innovative and creative avenues comes to rescue. This is the step where the frameworks i.e. the data gathering techniques mentioned in this book can be used to foster outside the box thinking using new ideas.

---

[7]. Ester Derby & Diana Larsen, Agile Retrospectives – Making Good Teams Great
[8]. https://www.amazon.com/Project-Retrospectives-Handbook-Team-Reviews/dp/0932633447

3. **Reflection on the emerging patterns:** As people post their ideas, the participants may group similar or duplicate ideas together. This grouping of similar data together will help in visualizing the emerging cluster of focus areas and how several issues are related. This step is best facilitated if participants can post their ideas on sticky notes for better visualization.

4. **Reflection on causes and options:** In this step, evaluate the data gathered in the previous steps to understand reasons behind what happened. Discuss the information gathered on the various categories and debate on them. For example, if one of the items cited in the previous step is to improve on time boxing, then the team discussions center point should be the causes and potential options to improve on the issue. An important point to remember is to focus on real problems and not just on the symptoms.

5. **Reflection on the action plan:** Here, focus on lessons learned from team discussions and what they wish to do differently so that the highlighted problems are not repeated. Ensure that you reiterate that retrospectives are about actions and outcomes, and not about finding faults with specific people. By the end of this step, the team must be in a position to summarize a few action items that they wish to follow up on in order to resolve identified impediments. These action items need to be achievable so that the team or individuals are able to work on them.

6. **Reflection on the priority of action items**: There might be situations where the team comes up with several action items at the end of an exercise. One way to avoid losing track is to prioritize these and pick up the most important items. Once the team finishes working on the priority items, they can pick the next set and so on, thereby working in an incremental manner.

7. **Reflection on the retrospective process**: The team reflects on what happened during the retrospective and offers feedback on areas of improvement in the process of conducting the retrospective. Ending with a positive note creates positive vibes! Thank everyone for their involvement, openness and the time spent.

* * *

9. ADVANTAGES

It is not a myth to say that everyone has the inherent capability of getting resourceful and creative. Teams can find their own answers, and can come up with diverse ideas when they collaborate as one team compared as against to one individual.

Retrospectives create a platform that allows teams and individuals to get wholesome, and helps them mirror their current journey, create a structure for teams to collaborate, and self-discover themselves. Once the team or any individual finds a solution by itself (or herself/ himself), they become more resourceful and this triggers curiosity that encourages them to explore limitless possibilities for their journey.

Retrospectives create passion for learning coupled with incremental accomplishments and this in turn fosters a growth mindset. According to Carols S. Dweck[9], this is vital for succeeding in today's fast-paced environment. Retrospectives aid in inducing a growth mindset by making incremental wins visible, challenges and obstacles evident, help people to plan, and take corrective actions. Retrospectives also help in reducing uncertainty by discovering and learning continuously.

It provides a platform for a facilitated learning where team members/ individuals can get curious about their state of journey, get compassionate, share observations openly and examine possibilities so that they come up with what works for them that is sustainable, and thus learn how to self-organize and self-manage.

Teams improve their interpersonal relationships, existing processes and tools. They also improve on various factors including performance, quality and productivity. Teams collaborate better as they openly voice their opinions, and listen to their peers. Retrospectives aid as energizers for teams when they debate and explore new ways to tackle problems, create a culture of continuous improvement wherein reflection becomes a norm rather than an exception.

This forum also serves as a great team bonding platform where a team can get to know each other personally. Retrospectives' benefits are holistic in the sense

---

[9]. https://en.wikipedia.org/wiki/Carol_Dweck

that they aid all the layers in the organization. The teams are continuously improving their course over a period of time, and this organically leads to the whole organizational set-up improving since the organizational impediments surface and get resolved during the course. Thus, the whole benefits as the team improves and finds better ways of working. The result is teams are motivated to build great products and the by-product of which is happy customers

Ultimately retrospectives lead to the whole business becoming more agile as they lend to improvements in key performance indicators such as getting more predictable, improving quality, improving team collaboration, faster go to market time, better communication between the team and business, and higher customer satisfaction.

Retrospectives lend to the agile principle - "At regular intervals, the team reflects on how to become more effective, and then refines and adjusts its behavior accordingly."

SITUATION SPECIFIC COLLABORATION FRAMEWORKS

CHAPTER 02

To catalyze conversations among team members and to bring back the efficacy of retrospectives, they need to be viewed from a different perspective. Teams need to do outside the box thinking and appreciate that these short gatherings need not be done by implementing the techniques or methods prescribed in the book but can be done by quoting some situational specific examples and case studies that would make the teams really think, and speak.

I will be sharing some metaphors that I have used for doing retrospectives. The intent of collating this tool kit is to generate a thought process among the readers to come up with their own situational specific ways for facilitation. Teams could pick the appropriate metaphor that suits them given the situation they are posed with. They can also customize the existing ones or create a new one.

What I am offering are diverse metaphors or analogies for different situations. These metaphors can be referred to as collaboration frameworks as they can be applied as is or can be tailored based on the context.

Most of the techniques will have the following format:

***

1. LOGISTICS AND ROOM SETUP

There are no specific requirements per say. Just an open space where team members feel relaxed to talk their mind.

A white board, if available would be great as most of these techniques work great when used in-person and can be visualized. A round table seating arrangement or an informal seating arrangement with bean bags will also do.

Ensure the room has enough wall space to write down things that come up for visualization. Let the room have enough space and ventilated so that the team members feel physically comfortable so that their mental state can be worked on. If teams are distributed, one can leverage online collaboration tools.

Make the meeting as informal as possible so that teams feel safe and feel free to open up. Have some food and snacks if possible, that will energize the team.

* * *

2. MATERIALS

Post-it notes (sticky notes) of different shapes and sizes, pens, flipchart paper, markers, sharpies, paper tape, scissors and white board. Throughout the book, I will be referring to some colors of sticky notes like red, green, blue or yellow. I would like to mention that participants can choose any color of their choice and need not restrict themselves to colors mentioned in the book.

In case you are running a large-team retrospective make sure the room is large enough for all participants where they can sit in smaller groups.

In case you are doing a remote retrospective for a distributed team, make sure you have video calling facility available and are using some online collaboration tools.

FRAMEWORK CLUSTERS

CHAPTER **03**

The frameworks i.e., the metaphors in this book have been grouped into logical clusters, however they can be used interchangeably in multiple contexts.

1. Address state of mind
2. Manage change
3. Nurture teamwork
4. Objective focused
5. Continuous reflection
6. Product leadership
7. Going beyond the routine
8. Personal reflection

Visualization helps us think laterally and represent our thought process better. Collaboration using visual metaphors leads to unexpected outcomes.

Don't be restricted by the metaphors and analogies mentioned in the book, these are dynamic and open to various forms of interpretation. Feel free to create your own sequence with these frameworks to help your team. Experiment and see how it works, there is nothing wrong in getting creative and learning new ways for a better tomorrow!

PART ONE

Nurture Team Work

NURTURE TEAMWORK

CHAPTER **04**

"None of us, including me, ever do great things. But we can all do small things with great love and together we can do something wonderful." – Mother Teresa

"No one can whistle a symphony. It takes a whole orchestra to play it." – H.E. Luccock

"Individually, we are one drop. Together, we are an ocean." – Ryunosuke Satoro

I am sure all of us watch or play some kind of sports and it is a known fact that if the team does not work well together, then irrespective of how good the players are the team will lose the game.

This concept applies to any industry. The team is the core for any successful accomplishment. Team dynamics need to be handled well. Working as one team and seeing through an organization's goal as a team goal is important in today's fast paced industry. It is difficult for teams to excel unless they know each other well and are able to think aloud, discuss with each other, ponder about their constraints and impediments that are holding them back. Psychological safety is one of the key attributes of a high performing team, it is imperative that we think about how such an environment can be fostered where a safe place is created for teams to open up.

The frameworks discussed here may help in teamwork:

- Shoot the ball
- Journey
- Highway drive

- Fly high
- Team values
- Rowing a boat
- Remote control
- Blind men and elephant
- Tandem bicycle

* * *

1. SHOOT THE BALL

Situation: In agile, cross-functional teams are important and they are the crux of delivering great products. It is important to understand the dynamics of an agile team in order to ensure they work as a single team instead of a group of people. At times, teams might focus on individual goals, instead of keeping their eyes on the team goal.

For instance, you have a team that works in separate functions – say, development and testing. If you need them to work as one cross-functional team, then this activity will help them visualize that structure. It will help in considering their current state and look at the steps they need to take to transform into a high performing team.

This exercise helps in focusing and driving the team towards a shared goal.

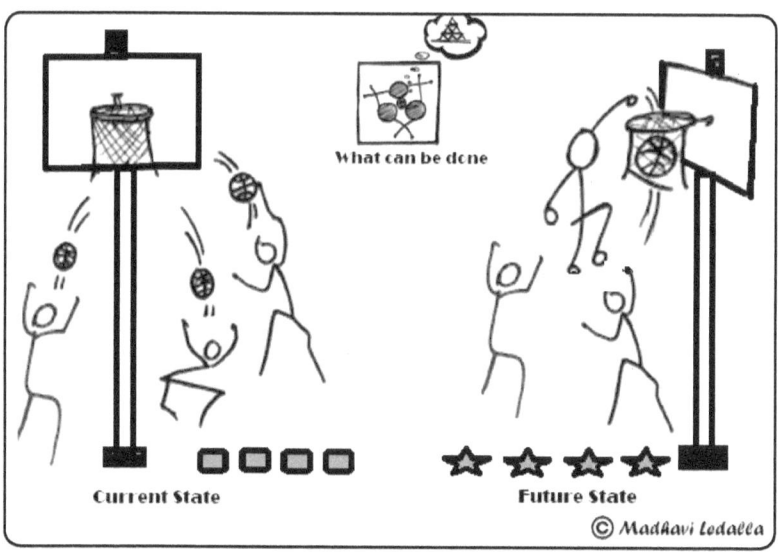

Let me tell you a story that will help you understand the agile team and mindset better. Basketball is one of my favorite sports, and I played the sport regularly with friends in school. Once, our team made it to the final in an interschool championship. But just the previous evening our coach had picked a new captain. This led to a bitter altercation – a war of words, and everyone's confidence in the team started to waver. I distinctly remember going to bed with a sense of fear and guilt.

After several years, I felt similar discomfort during a retrospective as I saw individual team members trying hard to put the ball in the basket on their own without keeping the entire team in mind.

On the day of the final match, despite the bitterness from the previous evening, my team stepped up, coordinated perfectly and we went on to win!

An agile team is like a team of basketball players and the sprints are like games. The team needs effective collaboration to win the championship. In a team of ace performers, each player is a great player with different expertise, but collective genius is what we seek. How do we ensure that the ace players are connected to the larger goal of winning the series?

The basketball analogy is relevant to the agile mindset where cross-functional teams need to learn to collaborate. How do I ensure that my team does not lose focus on the big picture during the sprint?

My high school basketball game drove me in the direction of a solution. I drew the picture above and told the team that the first scenario depicted individual team members trying to focus on their own goals, which would prevent them from meeting the team goal. I urged them to look in the direction of the shared team goals and asked them to think about things they could do to move the team from the situation on the left to the collaboration on the right. This method caught everyone's attention and made the retrospective lively and engaging.

Achieving success is not going to be easy. We have to learn to respect our differences and work closely as a team when there is a larger goal in sight.

This exercise helps in driving the team towards identifying bottlenecks and moving towards a shared goal. Debates and discussions are inherent here, which brings different perspectives to the foreground.

This exercise can also be used to address any generic problem apart from the cross-functional teams mentioned here. If you would like your team to move to a future state from the current state, this exercise could be useful for brainstorming.

Instructions

▸ Draw (or print out) the above picture on the whiteboard

▸ Hand out sticky notes and markers to the team

▸ Explain that the first scenario depicts individual team members or functions trying to focus on their own goals which will not always let them meet the team goal. Ask the team to list down the current attributes of the team on the left side of the picture. (Current State)

▸ Ask the team to imagine working towards a shared goal and list down the attributes of such a team on the right side of the picture. (Future State)

▸ Ask the team to note down the points that could potentially lead towards the second scenario (which depicts a shared goal) and put them in the middle of the picture.

▸ Follow this with a brainstorming session and talk about all the bottlenecks and reflect on the activities so that they can move from the first to second scenario

* * *

58 • Retrospectives for Everyone

2. JOURNEY

Situation: Sometimes, it is important to understand the big picture. You need to take stock of the team's progress so far to chart out the future course. If you would like to understand how the team's journey has been in the past sprints, this exercise will help. This exercise helps in visualizing the progress the team has made while addressing how the sprint could be made better in the future.

Whenever a team travels together, it builds a special bond among members. It creates memories and experiences that brings them closer. I use "team journey" as a metaphor in this exercise. Similar to an actual trip that a team takes, the sprints could be viewed as a journey too. The team could analyze data and experiences from the past sprints to discuss how the journey could be made better.

This exercise works well after the team has completed a minimum of four to five sprints so that they can visualize how they can work together.

Instructions

- Draw (or print out) the above picture on the whiteboard
- Hand out sticky notes and markers to the team
- Encourage the team to introspect and come up with impediments and enablers in the past sprints
- Drive them to adapt their discussion towards new ideas they wish to take up in the new sprint based on their previous sprints

* * *

3. HIGHWAY DRIVE

Situation: This exercise is particularly suited for ongoing projects. Owing to the length of the project, enablers and roadblocks are both common. This metaphor helps the team understand the driving forces and impediments in the project in particular, and the team at large.

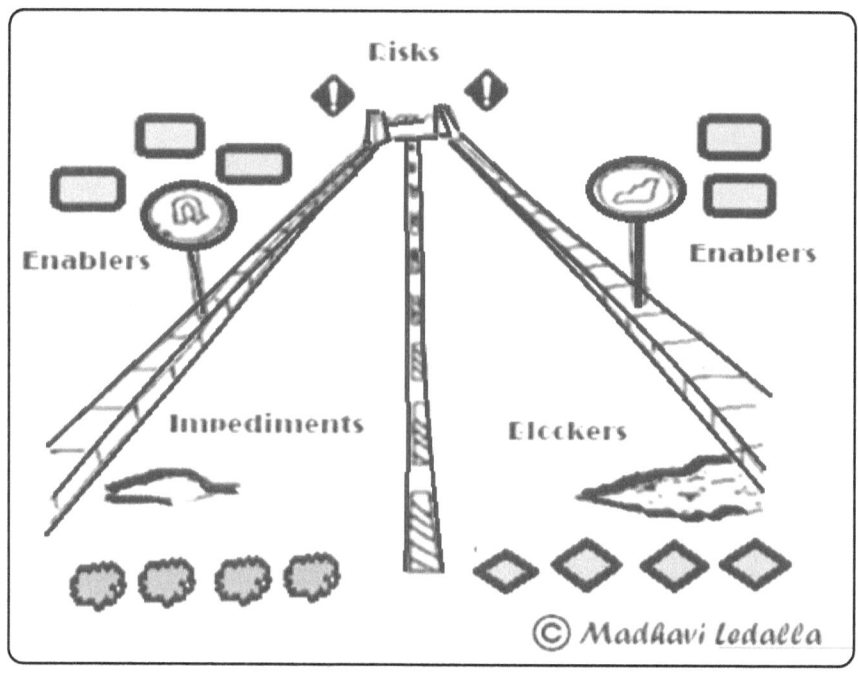

An ongoing project is like an ongoing road trip. While some stretches of the road are smooth and well-marked, there could also be stretches where the roads are bad, a sudden diversion or an out of place speed breaker that may slow you down. Despite these situations that are out of your control, how do you make your road trip smoother?

This retrospective technique uses "driving-on-a-highway" as a metaphor. Here, the road trip is the entire project. The team has started a road trip together, travelled some distance and there is still some distance to be covered before they reach their destination. Based on this journey, work with the team to identify enablers, blockers and threats, so that they can together arrive at how to continue the rest of the journey.

Let me explain the metaphor better. A part of the road trip (project) was smooth sailing with right signboards, supportive fellow drivers and indicators (enablers). However, team members suddenly encountered bad roads, ditches and a sudden diversion (impediments). Along their journey, they could have encountered major roadblocks like a fallen tree in the middle of the road that needed escalations. Sometimes, they faced an unexpected dead-end (threats) from which they could not move forward.

In short, for a good road trip (project) the team needs to arrive at:

- Enablers (signboards, indicators) that will help them reach their goal
- Blockers (bad roads, ditches, diversions) that are slowing them down
- Large impediments (the tree on the road) that need escalation
- Threats (dead-end) and risks

Instructions

- Print the above picture (or draw it) and put it up on the whiteboard
- Explain the context and ask the team to compare their project to a road trip. Ask them to visualize using the picture on the whiteboard
- Encourage the team to identify enablers, blockers, large impediments and threats
- How does your team visualize reaching the destination together?

* * *

4. FLY HIGH

Situation: Do you see several impediments that your team faces? However, you may also see that they do not take ownership of the issues and tries to pin the blame on the leadership. This exercise helps them reflect on what is within their scope and what is not.

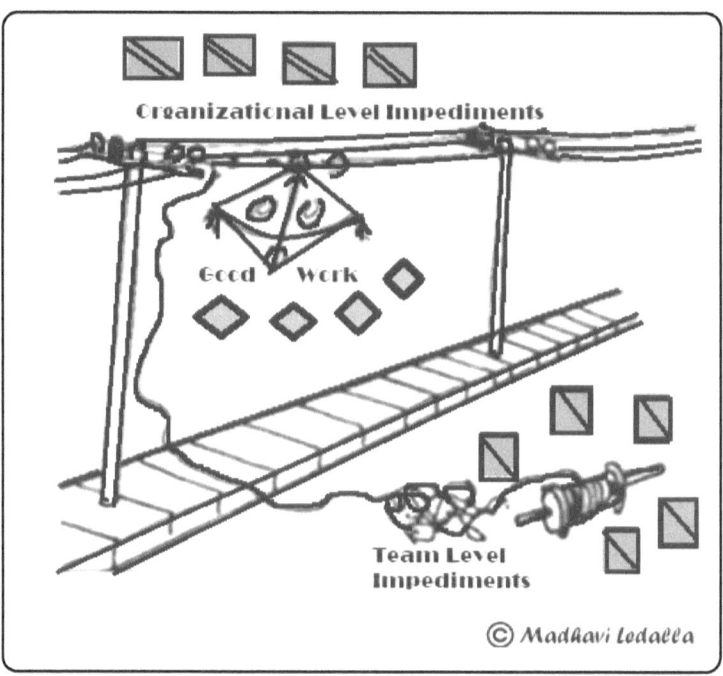

Let me explain this scenario with kite flying as an analogy. We fly kites every January during *Sankranti* – an Indian harvest festival. Often, if the string entangles itself on the ground, we try to remove it ourselves. However, sometimes the kite itself gets stuck on an electrical wire or the neighbor's rooftop. In such situations, we seek external help – either by using long sticks, or ask the neighbor permission to their rooftop – to remove the blockers.

During a retrospective close to *Sankranti*, with my kite flying still fresh in mind, it came to me that this experience was relevant to some of the scenarios we see with teams. I used it as an analogy with the team.

- Team level impediments are like the tangles on the ground – they can resolve it themselves if they work consciously in the right direction.
- Organization-level impediments are like the kite getting stuck on the neighbor's rooftop – they are beyond the team's scope and need to be escalated for resolution.

With this metaphor, I helped the team to:

- Identify the good work they have been doing and what they would like to continue doing
- Identify team-level impediments they could resolve by themselves, provided they worked towards them (similar to the entanglement I resolved myself)
- Identify impediments that needed escalation because they require support from the organization or senior management (similar to the kite getting stuck on the neighbor's rooftop)

Instructions

- Print the above picture (or draw it) and put it up on the whiteboard
- Explain the context and ask the team to compare their project to kite flying. Ask them to visualize using the picture on the whiteboard
- Encourage the team to identify the good work that they have been doing
- Help them identify blockers that they can resolve by themselves
- Identify impediments that require escalation
- Use different colored sticky notes for each of these categories and put them up on the board

* * *

5. TEAM VALUES

Situation: There are certain core Scrum values which encourage better working within the team. They are openness, courage, focus, respect and commitment. If you want to discuss with your team on the adoption of these values into the working culture, this technique will be of use to you.

These five core values[10] (as prescribed by the Scrum Framework) help teams adopt Scrum and create a supportive workplace. As a consequence, they work towards delivering quality results for the customers.

➢ Courage: The Scrum team has the courage to do the right thing, speak their voice and challenge the status quo if needed

➢ Openness: The Scrum team is open about their work, challenges and problems during the sprint

➢ Respect: The Scrum team respects each other, their values and strengths, and complements each other on the team.

➢ Commitment: The Scrum team commits to do their best in order to meet their sprint goal

➢ Focus: The Scrum team focuses on the sprint goal

This technique is a great exercise to check how well these values are imbibed into the team's mindset and the way they are working.

SCRUM VALUES	RATING (1-5)	REASON	DELTA (Improvements)
Courage			
Openness			
Respect			
Focus			
Commitment			

© Madhavi Ledalla

[10.] https://www.scrumalliance.org/about-scrum/values

Instructions

- Draw (or print out) the above picture on the whiteboard
- Hand out sticky notes and markers to the team
- On the sticky notes, ask the team to rate the sprint on the five Scrum values on a scale of 1 to 5 (1 being the lowest and 5 being the highest)
- Put these notes on the board and open a discussion with the team. The value that has the lowest rating could be the first checkpoint for inspection

* * *

6. ROWING A BOAT

Situation: Often we hear that there is no collaboration between members of the team. Individuals work in silos where they don't talk with each other. This technique addresses a situation like that. It is a focused technique to identify ways for the teams to be more collaborative.

A boat is often rowed along by a team. The entire team has to work together to dip and move their oars together. In Kerala, a state in the southern part of India, the canoe racing is a well-known annual sporting event. They have 30 to 35 meter-long "snake boats" with 64 or 128 paddlers on board depending on the size of the boat. The paddlers need to move in synchronous rhythm to ensure their team wins the race.

Much like the paddlers come together in a boat, teams need to foster collaboration to bring the best quality to their work. This visualization helps them understand collaboration better. In this exercise, ask the team to talk about ways in which they have collaborated with each other, how it helped and where could they improve?

> Accomplishment :
>
> How long :
>
> Slowed down :
>
> Did I get an oppopportunity to collaborate? YES/ NO/ HOW/ WHEN?
>
> Would collaborating more often speed up my accomplishment? YES/NO//HOW?
>
> © Madhavi Ledalla

Instructions

Pass on the sticky notes and ask the team to write their accomplishments. Example:

- ▸ Accomplishment: Completed sales target before the end of the month.

- ▸ Slow moving things: The customer service team could not process the final steps in the sale quickly.

- ▸ Opportunity to Collaborate: Yes, customer service team

- ▸ How: I worked alongside customer service to complete a particular group sale, which increased the sale number tremendously.

- ▸ What could be done differently to improve collaboration: The customer service process needs to be speeded up to help sales team meet targets faster.

Discuss each of these accomplishments with the rest of the team. At the end of this exercise the team should come up with a few common working agreements which will enable them to collaborate well in future sprints.

* * *

7. REMOTE CONTROL

Situation: If you would like your team to think of the big picture and how everyone's task is linked to the big picture, this exercise will help. It encourages you to consider what happens if any of the functions in the team isn't working properly and its impact on the team goals.

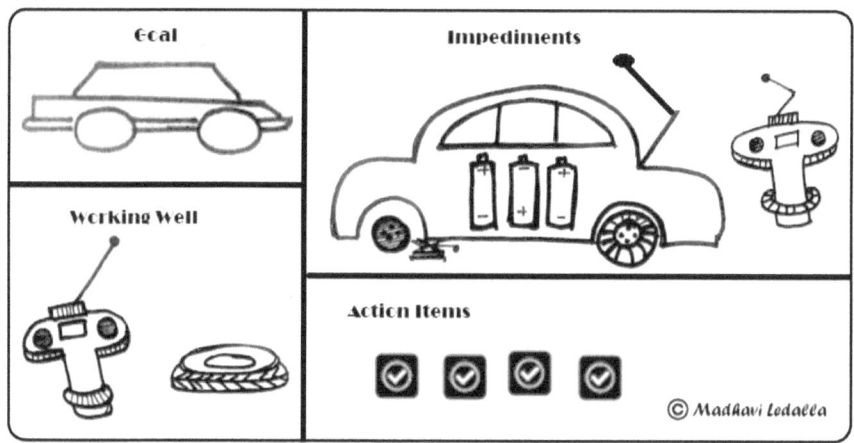

Once, while watching my nephew play with a remote-controlled car, I was intrigued by the process that was involved in controlling the car. He was focused, and there was perfect coordination of command and execution in his play. It was then I thought - why not gamify a retrospective using this very remote-controlled car?

Think about the car, it would work properly only if all its parts - the body, tires, batteries and the remote sensors - work together. Similarly, all the functions in an agile team need to collaborate and work in synchronization if the system must be successful. Only when all the functions of the team work in collaboration can we aim for teams to perform desirably.

For example, in a real estate company, it is important for the marketing, sales and customer service teams to come together to offer the best experience to the customer. Each team is in contact with the customer at various touch points, however the customer sees it as one company. So, only if all the teams work together, the customer experience translates well.

Instructions

- Draw or put up the above picture on the whiteboard
- Discuss with the team and identify the impediments that are hindering the work
- Identify some practices that are working well for the team, which they would like to continue doing
- Finally arrive at a few actions that would enable them to reach the goal

* * *

8. BLIND MEN AND THE ELEPHANT

Situation: Does your team have its own perception of a problem? Do you want to help team members think it through and make their perception visible? This exercise will help you get through to them.

I was intrigued by an ancient fable[11] that originates from the Indian subcontinent. In this story, a group of blind men perceive different parts of the elephant to be different things. Each of them only had access to a small part of the elephant and were conceptualizing the elephant with that knowledge. I wanted to use this metaphor with my team to help them visualize each other's perception, and how these perceptions would impact the team collaboration and dynamics.

Translating this to organizations worldwide, we realize that it is not the people who are blind, they just have a lens in front of their vision! For example, an organization with different functions can see issues through the lens of their position – development, release, pre-sales, post-sales, maintenance, finance,

---

[11.] https://en.wikipedia.org/wiki/Blind_men_and_an_elephant

operations or marketing. Essentially, the organization seldom notices the lens in front of every employee's eye.

In one team, I found that there were a few issues in on-boarding a new employee. Though each unit was doing their job thoroughly, when it came time to get feedback on the on-boarding process, it mostly stood at 8 on a scale of 1 to 10. Each group involved in the process believed and perceived that they did a great job.

In this team retrospective, I introduced the "blind men and the elephant" metaphor and asked each of the groups to describe from their perspective the experience and rate themselves on the on-boarding initiative and asked them to reason it out. After that I asked other groups to offer their rating to each other. This allowed them to see the outliers and discuss each other's viewpoints.

This exercise helped in getting several useful points out from different perspectives.

Instructions

- Draw the picture of the blind men and the elephant (or print it out) on the whiteboard. Explain the metaphor and give it the title of the problem to be solved. For instance, "On-boarding experience of a new employee" could be a title

- Talk about the problem on hand. Ask each of the responsible groups to rate their work on a scale of 1 to 10 and reason out the rating

- Take each item, discuss the reasoning and ask others how they would rate this item and what is their feedback

- Once you do this, the data and feedback reflect the pros and cons of the current issue at hand. The group would have enough clarity to improve or resolve the situation as they would be looking at the problem using different lenses that gives a varied perspective

* * *

9. TANDEM BICYCLE

Situation: If your team is working on moving from being individuals to a team, this exercise may be useful.

Individual Challenges
© Madhavi Ledalla

For the longest time I had the fear of riding a bicycle. Once on a vacation in Goa, I went out on a morning walk, and saw a tandem bicycle - a bicycle with four seats, where four people ride in tandem. My friends suggested that we try riding it. Although I was anxious, I thought that I had the support of others, and even if I don't pedal right, their riding would help me balance. I am glad I took the leap of faith and this ride turned out to be an unforgettable experience!

This experience came back to me when I heard a debate in my team. The team was stressed about a certain high priority issue they were trying to resolve. However, the development team was passing the ball to the testing team's court and vice versa. I could sense that the issue lay with individuals not owning work items and was sure if the entire team collaborates, they would excel. So, I described my tandem bicycle story to the team and facilitated a discussion.

Instructions

- Put up the picture above on the whiteboard. Distribute markers and sticky notes

- Encourage the team to share challenges that they face as individuals. Put these up on the side of the single-seater bicycle

- Discuss what the team can do to address these challenges. Put these up along the tandem bicycle on the board.

- Focus the discussion on how easy it is to achieve the target as a team rather than as individuals

PART TWO

Manage Change

MANAGE CHANGE

CHAPTER 05

"Agility is the ability to adapt and respond to change... agile organizations view change as an opportunity, not a threat." – Jim Highsmith

"Change is inevitable, change will always happen, but you have to apply direction to change, and that's when it progresses." – Doug Baldwin

"Without change there is no innovation, creativity or incentive for improvement. Those who initiate change will have a better opportunity to manage the change that is inevitable." – William Pollard

In today's fast paced world, change is inevitable. If we think I won't adapt, then we will be left behind in the game and will face a lot of difficulty to catch up with the market. One needs to be equipped, flexible and adaptable to understand why change is taking place and deal with it as it comes.

Change is built within our systems and processes as well. Every day we all know that we need to make some adjustments to deal with the demands as they come through and learn to embrace them.

The frameworks in this section can help you reflect on ways to deal with such situations, reflect on your change perception competence and how you can get better at dealing with changes as they come through.

Following frameworks are discussed in this section

- Snakes and ladders
- Holistic view
- Vicious cycle

- Chilly autumn
- Candle flame
- Scuba diving
- Complacent rabbit

* * *

Manage Change • 77

1. SNAKES AND LADDERS

Situation: If you have a highly energetic team that imbibes a competitive spirit, this game-based exercise helps to identify impediments and best practices to drive towards the sprint goal.

Snakes and Ladders[12] is a board game that originated in India and is regarded as a classic worldwide. This game usually involves two or more players, and they take turns to move up the grid by rolling the dice. On the way to the finish, the players meet hurdles in the form of snakes and opportunities in the form of ladders. When players encounter a snake, they are pushed down on the board, impeding their success. Whereas when players encounter a ladder, they tend to gain an opportunity to skip blocks and climb up on the board.

I was watching my darling daughters play this game with their friends at home. As a spectator of the game I realized that I could connect it to the

---
[12.] https://en.wikipedia.org/wiki/Snakes_and_Ladders

experiences in agile teams as they go through sprints to meet set goals. However, unlike in the game, it is not enough if one person wins. In an agile project, the game would be successful only when all the team members and functions climb the ladders and reach the sprint goal. Like in the game, the team will be met with sudden setbacks, but it is important to face them together and move on.

During one of our team retrospectives, I said, "Imagine that we are all playing a game of snakes and ladders. Can all of us reach the top at the same time?" Imagine the snakes are the impediments that teams face during their sprints. And ladders are the best practices we should continue following that would help us realize our sprint goal.

Gamification always works well in retrospectives since it makes the process exciting and encourages participation by allowing free flow of ideas which would not have come through conventional means.

Instructions

- Print (or draw) the above picture or use the actual board game of snakes and ladders and put it up on the whiteboard

- In the retrospective meeting, explain the context, and ask the team to compare their project to a game of snakes and ladders

- Imagine snakes to be impediments that teams face during their sprints. Think of ladders as best practices you should continue following, which could help you realize your sprint goal

- A fire torch could indicate precautionary measures to help the team improve and meet the sprint goal

- Ask them how they visualize reaching the finish line together?

* * *

2. HOLISTIC VIEW

Situation: An organization is characterized by structure, processes and strategy. If your team has systemic issues related to these, then this exercise gives you room to get the team and the leadership together under one roof for a discussion. These three elements are important factors for any organization that is on the path of transformation.

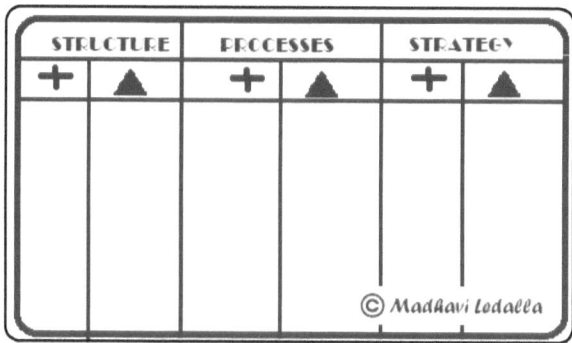

This technique brings out the underlying systemic problems in any team or organization that act as barriers in the agile approach. There could be several factors in the sprint that fall under these three categories. Based on the categories encourage the team to think of what is going well and what can be improved?

For example, under "Structure" a few things to consider could be cross-functional teams, functional teams, reporting structures and hierarchies. Similarly, under "Process", existing performance appraisal processes, and other technical processes such as testing, and release could be the points for discussion.

Instructions

▷ Print (or draw) the above table and put it up on the whiteboard. Distribute marker pens and sticky notes

▷ Explain the context to the team and encourage them to pitch their thoughts under each of the categories. Pick one category at a time

- ➢ Ensure every participant has answers to the following questions
    - What is going well in the three focus areas – Structure, Processes and Strategy?
    - What are the areas of improvement under these categories?
- ➢ Discuss the changes they are proposing to address the systemic challenges

※ ※ ※

3. VICIOUS CYCLE

Situation: At times certain issues crop up repeatedly causing a dent on the team's productivity. This exercise has been designed to identify such recurring issues that hamper a team's performance.

This exercise is an extension of a regular retrospective – start a regular retrospective, however this time add a specific quadrant called recurring issues along with the generic buckets. The team is usually aware of issues that pop up repeatedly, many of which could have been raised in the previous retrospectives.

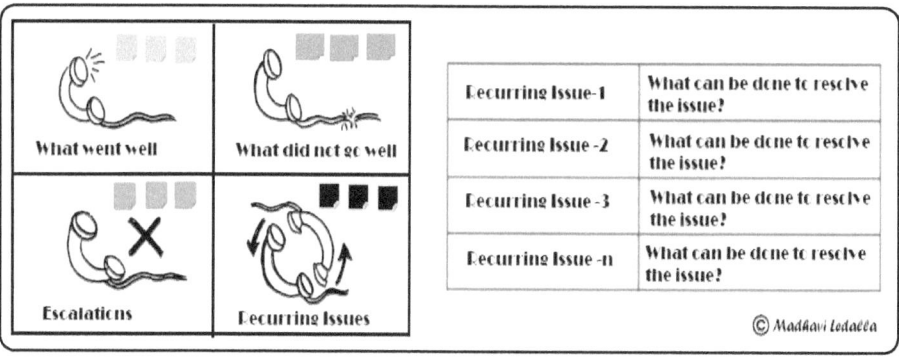

For instance, a phone conversation as shown in the above picture- how the conversation goes well and is clear on both ends, what happens when you face issues with the line being disturbed, cut or damaged? You then seek help from the customer support of the telephone operator and raise a ticket for repair. This is an issue that we may face often if the problem is not fixed properly.

Allow the team to think and list down the recurring issues, if the team is missing a few then any one can pitch in and remind the team of such issues. Once the recurring problems have been identified, you could use any technique to go to the root cause and fix it.

Instructions:

- Add a specific recurring bucket to the retrospective technique chosen on the whiteboard
- Discuss with the team and make notes of all the recurring issues one after another
- Discuss reasons for these issues to be arising repeatedly

※ ※ ※

4. CHILLY AUTUMN

Situation: Is your team doing well, do you think they could use a little push and get excited? This exercise will help you offer them just the right kind of additional support.

During our annual vacation, I was taking my morning stroll and soaking in the lovely autumn morning. However, it was colder than I expected. I guess I could do with another layer of clothing and enjoy the morning. As I stood under the tree to gaze at the beautiful surroundings, I started shivering in the cold.

During my session with a team, I narrated this experience and asked them to imagine the tree as their product and then asked them - what parts of their work made them happy and also urged them to look at the parts that called for extra support. Just like my scenario where I thought I needed more warm clothes to fight the cold weather.

Further, I asked them to list down things that could support their work, similar to the sweater, cap and gloves that I could have brought along.

The team came up with good points and we finally discussed what could be done from their end for the support systems to become a reality.

Instructions

- Put up the picture above on the whiteboard. Distribute markers and sticky notes

- Describe the experience of the walk on a cold autumn day. Imagine the tree as the product

- Ask the team to imagine what they like about their work so far and put it on the tree using sticky notes

- Discuss hindrances and put up these impediments outside the tree using sticky notes of another color

- Discuss the support systems that they believe will help them move ahead from these impediments. Put them up on sticky notes and put them up on the right side of the picture where you see the hat, gloves and jacket.

- Talk about how to make these support systems a reality

* * *

5. CANDLE FLAME

Situation: If you would like your team to envision detractors and promoters for your product, this exercise will be useful.

We often face power outages at our place of residence. There are times when we rely on the candlelight to complete our chores.

Sometimes when it gets windy, I cup my hands around the flame and ensure it does not extinguish. While working on an important task if the flame would extinguish due to the breeze or rain drops, I would get all worked up and annoyed.

I could connect this experience with the detractors and promoters in every product cycle. The detractors could be issues beyond your control, like a power outage that stops the work briefly or a competitor who launches the same product before you do, and promoters could be your product outlook and sales strategy.

In one of the retrospectives with a product group, I used this metaphor and asked the group to list out detractors and promoters for their product cycle during the initial development stages. This metaphor worked wonders with the team.

Instructions

- Put up the picture above on the whiteboard. Distribute markers and sticky notes

- Explain the candlelight metaphor and encourage the team to list out promoters of the product that will help market the product better

- Ask them to come up with detractors, i.e., impediments that will hinder the growth of the product

- Discuss the reasons associated with these detractors and what could be done to reduce their impact

* * *

6. SCUBA DIVING

Situation: If you want your team to think of tasks that need consistent focus throughout, this exercise will help you reach out to them.

Scuba divers carry oxygen tanks throughout the dive. It acts as their life support system under water. There are similar support systems that every team need. For example, teams need to continuously focus on removing technical debt and may need to continuously integrate their code multiple times a day to ensure quality delivery.

In one of the team retrospectives where the team was not focused on these live support systems, I used the metaphor of scuba diving. This encouraged the team to assess what they need to continuously practice in their regular work.

Instructions

➢ Put up the above picture on the whiteboard. Distribute markers and sticky notes

➢ Explain the metaphor. Ask the team about tasks that need a continuous attention without exception. For instance - like breathing without an oxygen tank underwater in impossible. Put these on sticky notes and put them on top of the cylinder. Discuss what they should do to start focusing on these continuous tasks, i.e., what they need to inhale to start their dive

▷ Discuss what they need to exhale, i.e., what they should stop doing, to remove the impediments they are facing that would help them focus on such ongoing work

* * *

7. COMPLACENT RABBIT

Situation: Don't we all know the famous fable of the rabbit and the tortoise[13], where the tortoise plans well and wins the race, the rabbit loses because of its overconfidence and lack of dedication and a well thought plan.

During a sprint you may notice that the team is functioning in an ad hoc manner, lacking focus on the goal and working mechanically. Given this situation, the complacent rabbit will act as a good metaphor to get the team going.

There will be instances where you see team members spontaneously taking some decisions or doing things without much thought that may become hindrances in the long run. For example, let's consider a team of lecturers who are planning their curriculum and administrative work for the quarter. There could be a situation where due to events, unexpected holidays or emergencies the teachers could not complete their task and ask the students to learn the lessons themselves or skip parts of the curriculum all together. The main problem with this setup is that the students will lose out in quality education in the long run. A possible solution could be that the lectures plan in advance and make use of technology to provide online lectures during emergencies.

[13.] https://www.moralstories.org/the-rabbit-and-the-turtle/

Instructions

- Ask any team to draw this picture or take a print out and stick it on the board
- Ask the team to think through the goals and specify on the end line
- Add as many rabbits as they can for ad hoc or neglected decisions that they have taken. For further visualization, you could also add two separate colored sticky notes one for the ad hoc and another for neglected decisions
- Ask them to think of the things that they have thought well and add as many tortoises as they can
- Then ask them to discuss what can be done to see more of tortoises and less rabbits in the future, and come up with action items. While they discuss about rabbits, ask them to specify the action items on another sticky note and post it right next to the ad hoc and neglected decisions with what can be done about it

PART THREE

Product Leadership

CHAPTER 06

PRODUCT LEADERSHIP

"The essence of strategy is choosing what not to do." – Michael Portere

"When the wind blows, some people build walls, others build windmills." – Chinese proverb

"People think focus means saying yes to the thing you've got to focus on. But that's not what it means at all. It means saying no to the hundred other good ideas." – Steve Jobs

A product leader is eventually responsible for the success or failure of a product, they play a key role in realizing the company's vision and hence they are often referred to as a single wringable neck. They interact with users and other stakeholders, champion the product, facilitate the product decisions and maximize the value of the product. This is no mean feat. Often 20% of the features deliver 80% of the value and identifying this 20% is not easy. Product leadership should be able to think through the vision, visualize how the product can stand out in the market and survive the competition.

The frameworks in this section may help trigger discussions and thought processes among the product group and team members and be instrumental in driving the product thinking mindset.

- Garden your thoughts
- Magic lamp
- Dream product

- Nurture the plant
- Product eel
- Mushroom cloud
- Time travel

* * *

Product Leadership • 95

1. GARDEN YOUR THOUGHTS

Situation: The project is moving at an expected pace. However teething issues pop up, which have not been addressed appropriately. If not tackled with a permanent solution they can potentially manifest themselves in a bigger way in the future.

This exercise helps the team identify the issues and nip them in a bud to keep the project on the right track. This exercise works well for ongoing projects.

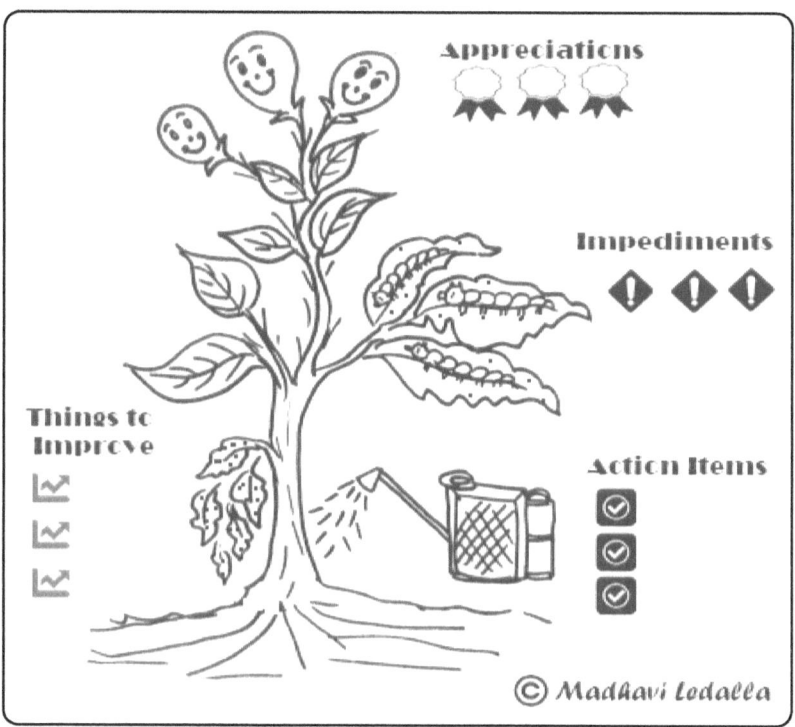

On a relaxed Sunday morning, as I was watering my plants, I noticed insects on some of the leaves. I decided to let them be and ignored them for a few days. However, after a few days I noticed that the insects started infesting other plants as well.

Our work also may indicate similar early stage threats which are often ignored. It might so happen that small issues that were ignored as they were not urgent may pile up into being one of the biggest hurdles in the project. In a collaborative working environment, any small issue left unattended may end up slowing down the entire value chain. What could have been avoided will become an impossible problem.

While conducting a retrospective with teams, I drew a picture of a plant on the board. "Look," I said, "this plant is our project, and I would like us to do the following things." Think of all the bottlenecks that, if not addressed, could eventually eat us up like hungry worms that devour fresh leaves. Identify best practices that really worked well for us, like watering the plant, adding manure, providing efficient sunlight and so on. Realize collectively what it is that we want to try differently to e stay on the right track, just like how we might need to inject fertilizer into the soil, act upon the early signs of worms, keeping the area clean. Lastly, identify potential areas of improvement as we would tend to the drooping leaves on a plant.

This situation is particularly relevant to agile teams because collaboration is crucial for the health of agile life cycles, any unattended issue slows down the entire value chain.

Instructions

- Print the above picture (or draw it) and put it up on the whiteboard
- Explain the context to the team and ask them to visualize with the help of the picture
- Encourage them to identify bottlenecks, best practices and areas of improvement
- Collectively arrive at action items that will help them stay on track in the project

***

2. MAGIC LAMP

Situation: Didn't we all grew up loving the fairy tales? Talking about them even today awakens the inner child in us.

Everyone knows the timeless Middle-Eastern fable *'Aladdin and the Magic Lamp'*. I enjoyed watching it as a kid and watched with equal enthusiasm with my kids. I would get extremely excited when Aladdin would rub the magic lamp and genie would appear and grant Aladdin his wishes. I thought the concept of the magic lamp could be used to discuss a new product development by my team.

I put up a picture of Aladdin and Genie and asked my team to come up with three wishes they wanted Aladdin to grant for their dream product. The team quickly got the message and collated an entire wish list for the success of the project.

You could use this concept for team retrospectives as well. Ask your team for three wishes that would ease their work and add value to the big picture of the project. Feel free to customize the concept and build on it as it can be useful in different scenarios.

Instructions

- Put up the picture of Aladdin and the magic lamp on the board
- Discuss with your team about their wish list for the product. Put these up on the board
- You could also vary the exercise slightly by asking each team or stakeholders to come up with their own magic lamp and wish list. Consolidate these into one list eventually

※ ※ ※

3. DREAM PRODUCT

Situation: Does your team build a product? Do you want your team to identify the difference between the need-to-have features and nice-to-have features? This exercise will help you work with your team.

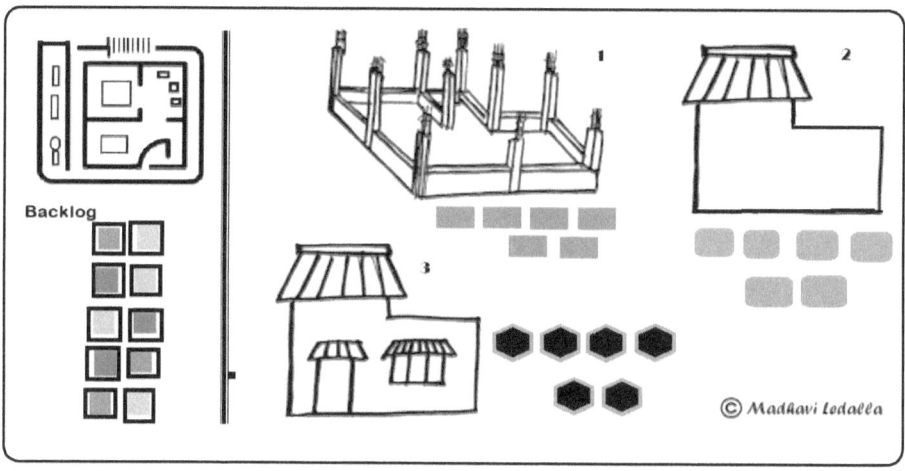

A few years ago, while constructing my house, I remember working with an architect to draw up plans based on dependencies and design. We began with a high-level plan and initially constructed the foundation and pillars. These are the major need-to-have features in a house. After this, we constructed the walls and the rooms. The interiors soon followed.

During a retrospective, the team was debating on the product features to be built. I used the metaphor of constructing a house and compared it to the product we intended to build. Based on the dependencies and priority, we divided the backlog into stages and areas, like the construction of a house.

The team could relate to this metaphor easily as most of us are familiar with the concept of constructing a house. You can add more layers/phases to this picture to expand it as needed.

Instructions

- Draw the picture above (or print it out) on the whiteboard. Describe the metaphor to the team

- The blueprint of the house resembles your team's high-level plan or the backlog

- The first picture, i.e., the foundation represents the need-to-have features. Ask the team to discuss these. Write them on sticky notes and put them on the board

- Discuss features which are important and must be built on top of the foundation. Put them up on sticky notes on the board

- Discuss features which are nice-to-have, like the woodwork in a house and put sticky notes on that part of the board

- Once this snapshot is done, look at how the features are distributed and reorder them accordingly

* * *

4. NURTURE THE PLANT

Situation: You need to inculcate the value of - Never fail the customer. To avoid the pitfall of ignoring the customer's needs, this exercise will come handy and help the team reflect.

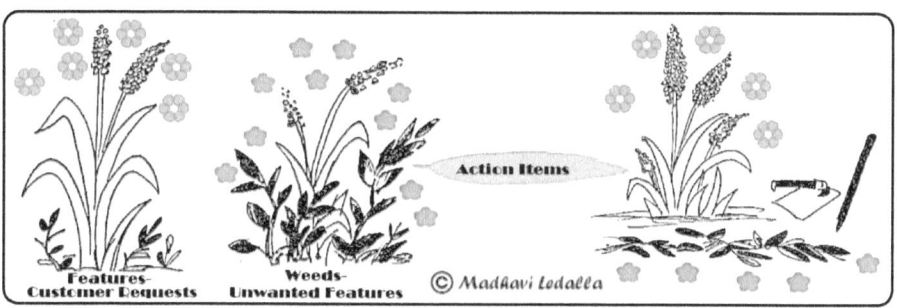

I am a gardening enthusiast and a dear friend of mine shares this passion with me. She had multi coloured crotons in her garden and I just loved to spend time with all her colourful plants. During my recent visit I noticed that several weeds had grown around the plants. My friend told me that she was too caught up with other things and couldn't tend to her garden.

Around the same time, I was working with a team that never interacted with customers and built whatever they thought was right. That is when I could visualize that their product had a possibility of ending up in the same situation as my friend's garden - more unwanted features (weeds) and less customer needs fulfilled - if they continued to work in the same way.

I used my friend's garden as a metaphor and discussed the team's situation. We put up red sticky notes on features that they had built by themselves and green sticky notes on features that the customer wanted. Soon it was obvious that the red features dominated over the green ones.

After a discussion on why the team proceeded the way they did so far, we had several interesting insights. Lack of skill set was a pain point that popped up during the discussion along with lack of clarity on product roadmap.

We used these insights to discuss how the team was going to proceed further - how they were going to weed out the unwanted plants and grow their crotons better.

Instructions

- Put up the picture above on the whiteboard. Distribute markers and sticky notes

- Explain the metaphor to the team. Ask the team to list out customer-requested features on green sticky notes on the board along the croton plants

- Tell the team to list features that they built on their own on red sticky notes along the weeds on the board

- Give them some time to visualize the final situation - what does the picture depict? Is the product healthy and is it aligned to customer needs or not? If not, what are the implications of doing so?

- If the reds are more than the greens and it seems like the product is in a problem area, brainstorm ways to rescue the product

* * *

5. PRODUCT EEL

Situation: If you want your team to think outside the box and come up with exceptional ideas then this technique might help!

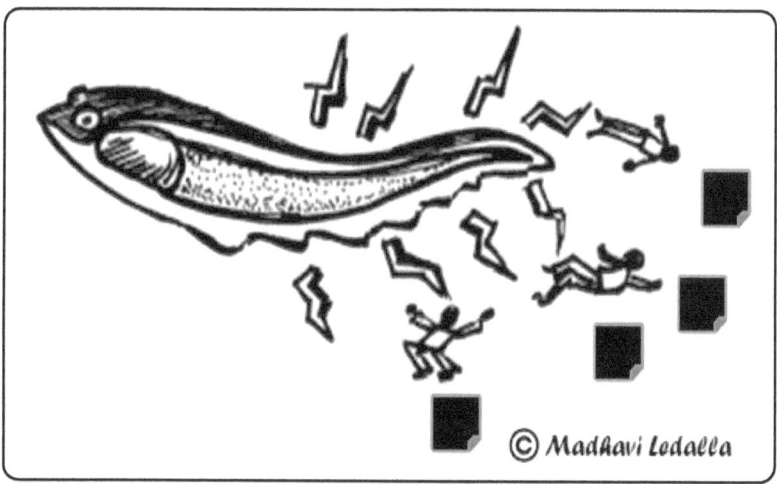

I was on a vacation in Singapore and while doing touristy things I visited one of the largest aquariums and came across a fish named "Electric Eel", also known as the "Shocking fish", it is a giant fish that emits volts of electricity and can kill people. I could not remove the image of the shocking fish from my mind.

One day I saw a team discussing the cutthroat competition in the market and they were debating on what they can add to the product that will enable them to fight the competition.

Suddenly I could relate this to the shocking fish that has the ability to kill others! Spontaneously I described the unique trait of this fish, and I asked, "What is that one shocking feature you want to build that would kill all your competitors in the market?" The metaphor brought forth a lot of discussions and some great ideas.

When you use real world examples, it always creates wonders!

Instructions

- Put up the picture above on the whiteboard and describe the shocking fish. Distribute markers and sticky notes

- Encourage the team to come up with ideas that create an experience similar to that of the electric eel in the market

✳ ✳ ✳

6. MUSHROOM CLOUD

Situation: Do you have a big project coming up that requires in-depth thought? This could be a new feature to your product or a new product for which your marketing team has to build a brand. In such a situation, it helps to break down every big item to smaller chunks and focus on the smallest of the details.

I was watering the coconut tree in my backyard; I saw a few mushrooms crop up on the soil. Then after a few days I saw a few baby mushrooms pop out from the big ones and then they started multiplying. These mushrooms reminded me of a team which was in the initial stages of product development.

So, in one of their team retrospectives I used this concept. I asked the team to break their project down from a big mushroom and branch out into smaller ones. Eventually the baby mushrooms are the ones who will have to be rooted to ensure product delivery.

Instructions

- Put up the picture above on the whiteboard. Distribute markers and sticky notes

- Ask the team to come up with one big mushroom that is their product/feature

- Encourage them to add baby mushrooms cropping out of the big one to represent the breakdown of bigger items to smaller items. The bigger mushrooms may represent the big features and the outermost baby mushrooms represent the smaller actionable items

- Discuss the smallest mushrooms as their deliverables

* * *

7. TIME TRAVEL

Situation: If you would like your team to differentiate between what they need to focus on short term, long term and the very long term, then this exercise will be interesting.

Time travel is a metaphor to describe various objects that get visibility while going up from the Earth to the outer space. Initially when we are on the Earth, objects like houses and trees are visible. As we travel higher, we see clouds. Based on how long you have travelled, you see objects at different levels.

I felt this exercise could be used to prioritize work. "Now" refers to what you need to build first to prepare the first cut of the product. "Near" refers to the next set of features that you should work on. For example, this could be in a time frame of six months. "Very far" refers to items in the long term - for example, these could be plans and goals over the next two years. The time boxes could vary based on the context.

Essentially this metaphor is an engaging way to explore the journey of the product.

Instructions

- Put up the picture above on the whiteboard. Distribute markers and sticky notes. Describe the concept of time travel
- Title the rocket with the name of your product
- Ask your team to come up with features for 'Now', 'Near' and 'Very Far'
- Discuss the evolution of the product over the years

PART FOUR

Objective Focused

OBJECTIVE-FOCUSED

CHAPTER 07

"Success is the progressive realization of a worthy goal or ideal."
— *Earl Nightingale*

"One way to keep momentum going is to have constantly greater goals". — *Michael Korda*

We all know that setting goals and working to achieve them gets challenging if we are not focused. There are many situations where we set up goals for ourselves, but pay little or no attention to the follow ups required in the execution.

Here when I say a goal, I am referring to what objectives a team sets so that everyone has a shared understanding of their purpose and work as a team towards realizing the same.

The frameworks in this section help you to think through the drivers for reaching stated goals and difficulties or bottlenecks that are causing you to drift away from your objectives.

- The bottleneck
- Climbing a mountain
- Spotlight
- Retro clock
- Bow and arrow
- Rapid fire
- Perfect day
- Speed up

***

1. THE BOTTLENECK

Situation: Do you sense a slowdown in the delivery pipeline of your project? This activity will help visualize which step in the workflow is suffering and what are the bottlenecks. Identifying the bottlenecks and dealing with them will help in optimizing the workflow.

STAGE 1		STAGE 2		STAGE 3		STAGE 4	
Cloud 9	Hell	Cloud 9	Hell	Cloud 9	Hell	Cloud 9	Hell
ACTION PLAN		ACTION PLAN		ACTION PLAN		ACTION PLAN	

© Madhavi Ledalla

Let me explain this in simpler terms – back in high school, we were always told that neglecting even one subject could impact the final grade sheet. So, if a child does well in Mathematics, but does not do well in History that would impact the overall grade.

Similarly, in a workflow that involves multiple stages – analysis, development, review, testing and deployment, if you experience a bottleneck in any one stage, this will have an impact on the overall delivery. This exercise will help identify and resolve these bottlenecks.

Instructions

- Draw the table above (or print it out) on the whiteboard. Replace Stage 1... to Stage n with the names of the actual workflow stages relevant to your project
- Hand out sticky notes and markers to the team
- Give the team a few minutes to think of the best and worst moments, the Heaven and Hell moments in each stage

- Ask the team to individually put down these heaven and hell moments on the sticky notes, and stick them on the relevant columns on the table

- If you see a cluster of sticky notes on a particular hell column, it would indicate a bottleneck that needs to be discussed and debated. Discuss with the team and encourage them to identify more bottlenecks, and look at ways to resolve them

***

2. CLIMBING A MOUNTAIN

Situation: At times teams work well together, however they tend to ignore certain risks that are going to affect them in the future. Without being prepared for these impediments, the team's direction towards the end goal will be diverted.

This activity helps the team reiterate what their goal is, arrive at enablers and impediments based on the previous sprint, and envision risks they foresee. Often, these risks could create serious consequences.

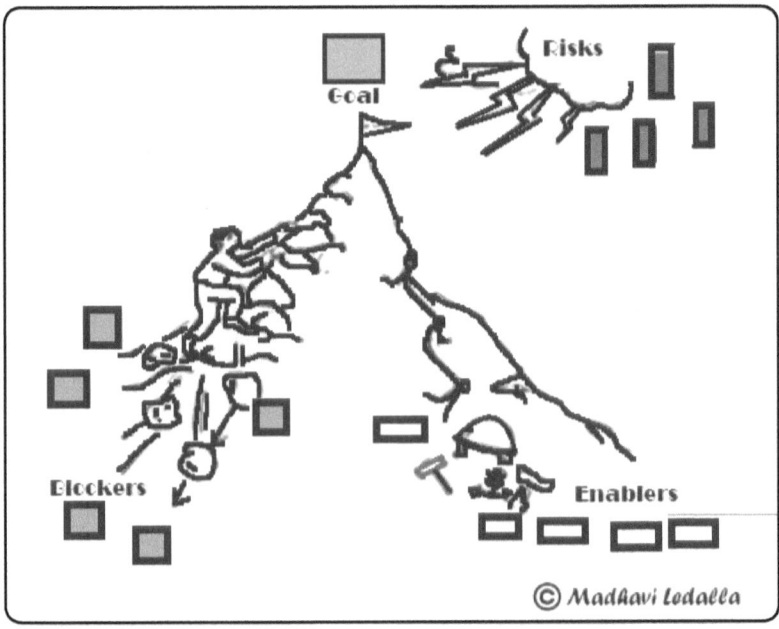

Mountaineering is an adventurous activity; it tests your strength and that inherently involves a lot of learning. While climbing a mountain, there are terrains where you will need the right gear to support the climb, and there are sudden changes in the weather that could put a premature stop on the journey uphill. Similarly, for a project there are hurdles and risks that slow us down, and there are also enablers that help the team move towards the sprint goal.

Using climbing a mountain as a metaphor, the team identifies slippery slopes (impediments), right gear like boots, helmets, torch lights, walking sticks and ropes (positive factors), and weather changes (risks and threats) to plan areas of improvements for the next sprint.

Instructions

- Print the above picture (or draw it) and put it up on the whiteboard.
- Explain the context and ask the team to compare their project to climbing a mountain. Ask them to visualize using the picture on the whiteboard.
- Encourage the team to identify impediments, risks and driving forces.
- Use different colored markers and sticky notes for better visualization.
- Discuss the data points to overcome the impediments and risks.

* * *

3. SPOTLIGHT

Situation: Do you want your team to make certain changes so that there is an immediate impact on certain key areas like quality delivery, zero-defects or 100% code coverage? This exercise helps the team focus on areas that need attention right away.

This exercise works better when the team has finished a significant number of sprints so that they can visualize some key focus areas. This is recommended but not mandatory.

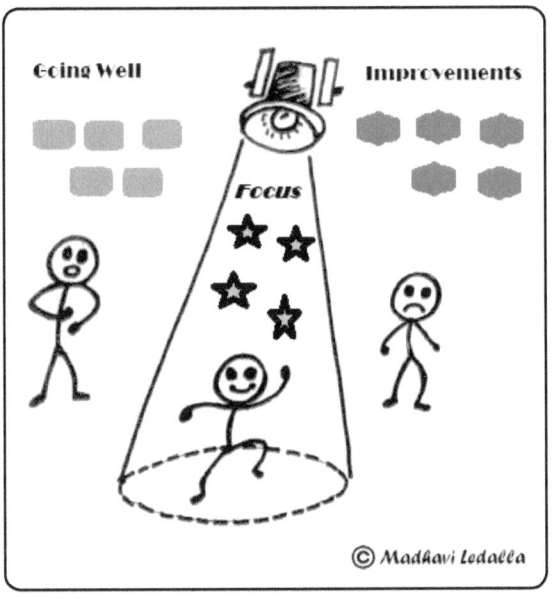

In my experience, I have learnt that adding a specific focus quadrant helps a lot. For example, you are part of a recruitment team and there is an immediate need to add 50 new people to the organization in three months. The current recruitment cycle is two months, so how will you reduce this time to two weeks to meet the demand? In such situations, you can add a focus quadrant and ask the team to come up with items that need immediate focus. This will drive your team to meet the larger requirement. We could use this focus quadrant for any item that requires immediate attention and emphasis.

Instructions

▷ Print (or draw) the above quadrant on the whiteboard. Distribute marker pens and sticky notes.

▷ Explain the context to the team and ask the team members to think about what part of their work is going well – what did they like in the current sprint? Also encourage them to think of improvement areas.

▷ Then, move on and mention that the focus area for the current sprint is "xxx" and ask them to think about how they could work towards this focus area. For example, if the focus is to speed up the recruitment cycle, then what would the team like to do so that their recruitment speed improves?

* * *

4. RETRO CLOCK

Situation: Do you foresee several areas of improvement for a team? Do you want to come up with an actionable working plan for the next few sprints? This exercise will come to your rescue.

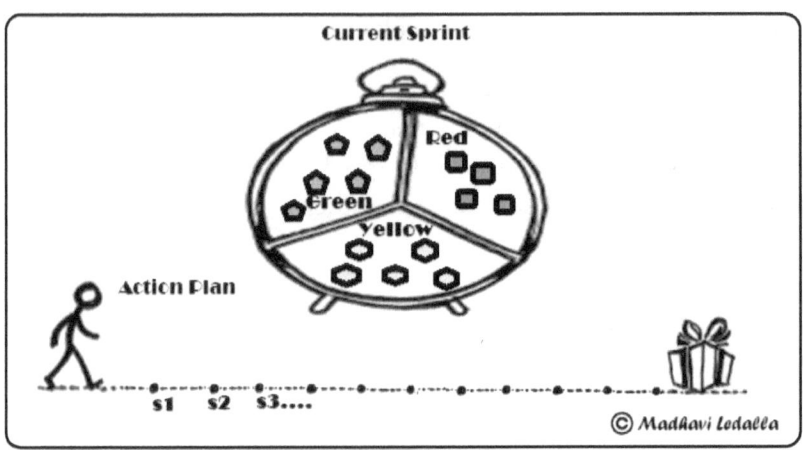

During the team retrospective, there could be action items spanning across multiple sprints that arise based on the current sprint's performance. For instance, if the team is working towards increasing their sales target by 50% in the next quarter, actionable items could span across many sprints and cannot be done in a single sprint. In such situations you can ask the team to come up with an ideal working plan to address these actionable items that span across multiple sprints.

Instructions: (This is a two-step process)

Step 1: Current Sprint Retrospective

- Print (or draw) the above picture and put it up on the whiteboard
- Conduct a retrospective of the current sprint
- Identify the red/green/yellow areas of the sprint and note them inside the clock using sticky notes. Green indicates areas which are going well Yellow indicates areas that need improvement. Red indicates problematic areas
- Come up with action items to work on the items in yellow and red

Step 2: Chalk out a Working Plan

In case, the action items are big tasks such as achieving 100% code coverage, zero priority one defects, or automation, they may take multiple sprints for completion. Such items can be visualized using the timeline action plan part of the picture.

- Pick up the action item you arrived at in the previous step
- Jot down how you want to achieve this goal in "x" sprints based on your business goals
- List down the plan of action in each sprint and make notes on what the team would like to achieve in each sprint
- Discuss each action item that spans across multiple sprints using this method

This method may help the team to come up with a long-term working plan

* * *

5. BOW AND ARROW

Situation: Does your team find it difficult to deal with changes? This exercise will get them on board with the change sooner!

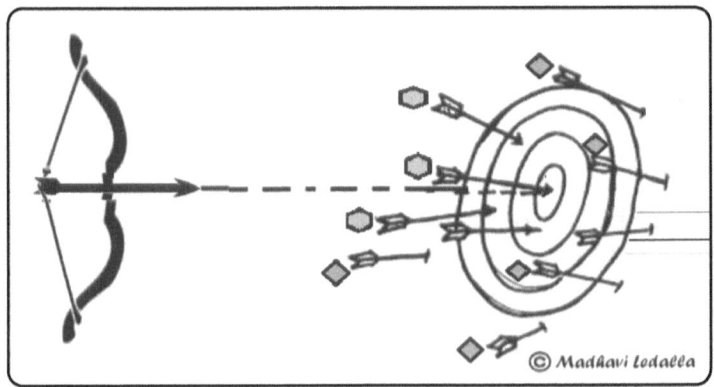

A team I worked with often complained that the scope of work changed making it tough for them to meet their initial goals. Change is constant and teams need to learn to adapt.

During a team outing, I thought about reaching out to the team. We were at a recreational center and decided to try archery. In my initial few attempts, I got a few arrows on the board and few outside. As I took time to reflect on what I did, I realized that I was unable to pay attention due to the distractions in the surroundings. After a few rounds, I made some changes including changing the shooting angle, choosing a bow of lighter weight and using back support - these helped me nail the target

With the help of this anecdote to help the team visualize their current state. I explained to the team how I played the game and what changes I made that helped me hit the target. I drew the picture on the board, titled it with the team goal, and asked the team to draw arrows that helped them meet the goals and those that did not. Finally, we discussed the arrows that went outside - those that did not help meet the goal. Each arrow represented a change request.

Instructions

▷ Put up the picture above on the whiteboard. Title the board at the center with the team goal. Distribute markers and sticky notes.

▷ Ask the team to add arrows to indicate changes made to the project. Create one arrow for each change.

▷ Arrows which go towards the goal are those that have a positive impact or zero impact on the goal. Arrows that go outside the board are those that caused forecasted commitments to be missed.

▷ Discuss why the change was introduced and what can be done to minimize such changes. If it is a reasonable change that is inevitable discuss ways of handling them better. This will give great insights to the leadership to help them understand the lasting impact of changes.

※ ※ ※

6. RAPID FIRE

Situation: If your team is pressed with time and you want to gamify the retrospective and encourage them to jump on to the priority items, then this activity will be the right fit.

Rapid fire is useful when you want to complete a retrospective quickly.

Please note that it should not be a regular practice to use 'rapid fire' as the only retrospective method. This is meant only for situations where the team is really crunched for time.

Instructions

- Ask each team member to come up with two items, one per sticky note for discussion.
- Gather the items and ask the team to vote up the items. Every individual gets three votes.
- Pick three items that got the maximum votes for the retrospective discussion.
- For each item, discuss what went well and what the issues were. Come up with solutions about what needs to be done so that the same problem does not repeat in the next sprint.

***

7. PERFECT DAY

Situation: Sometimes your team may be spending a lot of time on certain non-priority tasks. Help them identify this and rectify it using 'Perfect Day' as an exercise.

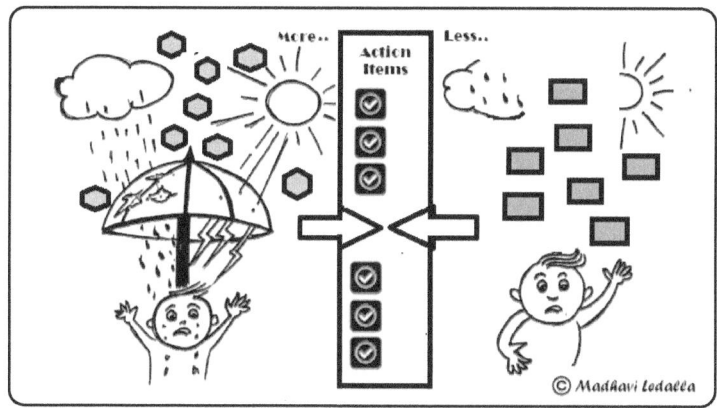

It is good if the Sun shines just enough and it is good if the rain pours just enough. However, if the temperature keeps soaring or if it rains continuously, it makes us uncomfortable and it also hampers our daily schedule. Similarly, we can notice that we could experience the same situation at work as well, where there are teams who work a lot on a few tasks and neglect the other tasks. For example, I had a team that was doing multiple levels of code reviews - first with peers, then with the team and then across teams. Another example could be multiple levels of approval processes for getting access to a database environment.

Use this metaphor to help the teams break this cycle.

Instructions

➤ Depending on the season, draw an appropriate picture on the whiteboard. Distribute markers and sticky notes

➤ Explain the metaphor. Ask the team members how they would feel if they were to experience soaring temperature outside or extremely heavy rainfall

- ▶ Understand from them, if they spend a lot of time doing certain tasks. Give each team member a few minutes and note their responses on a sticky note. Put it up on the left side of the board

- ▶ Similarly ask the team to note tasks that they don't spend enough time on. Put these sticky notes up on the right side of the board

- ▶ Discuss what could be done to balance out the workload and how they can focus on essentials, make a note of the action items in the middle of the picture for action and implementation.

※ ※ ※

8. SPEED UP

Situation: Sometimes a team could be great in a few areas and may need improvement in others. If you want your team to think and assess their situation, and understand where they want to get to, this technique will help. It pushes the team towards a holistic focus.

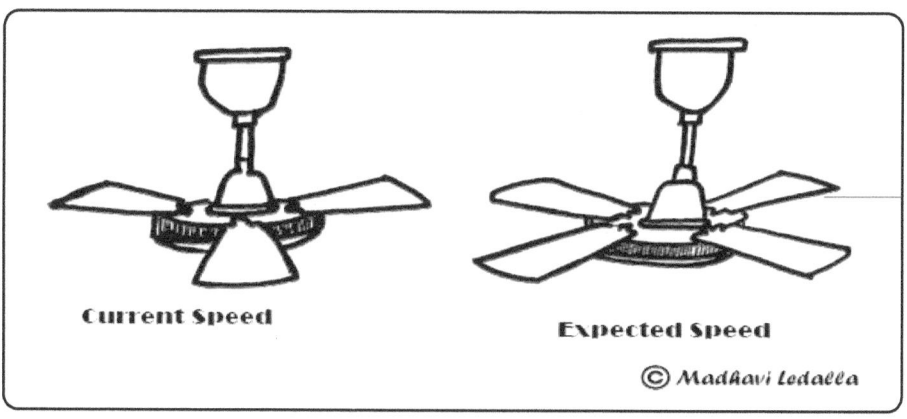

Often, when I am immersed in deep thoughts, I keep staring at the blades of the fan in my living room. During winters when it tends to get a little cold, I keep adjusting the speed of the fan. In the tropical environment I live in, it just takes a few minutes to feel warm again. On a particular day I was restless that day and changed the speed of the fan multiple times.

Those series of repetitive actions reminded me of my team - they were excelling in some parts of their work and lagging in others. We were trying to arrive at improving performance. So, the question that popped was - what speed was my team performing at?

We worked to understand their current speed and we also spent time on understanding the speed that the team needed to work on to reach their goal. Just like the different blades of the fan operate at the same speed, all parts of the team also need to work together at one speed.

Instructions

- Draw a picture of a fan, as shown above (or print it out) on the whiteboard

- Define the blades, i.e. categorize them as the major pieces of team work/or major functions. In a marketing team, this could be business development and sales team support, creatives and communication, strategy, content and social media marketing, advertising and promotions

- Let the team define what their current speed is. Ask them to add what are the current attributes that help them function at the current speed. Let them note these on sticky notes and categorize them according to the sections (blades). For instance, your team may excel in the sales team support that they offer, but lag severely behind in content marketing initiatives

- Now, let the team define what is the maximum speed they would like to function at? Encourage them to think about the characteristics of such a team? Also, ask them to discuss steps they need to take to speed up to reach their expected speed. Let them note these on sticky notes and place the items on the blades based on identified categories

PART FIVE

Continous Reflection

CHAPTER 08

CONTINUOUS REFLECTION

"It does not matter how slowly you go as long as you do not stop."
— *Confucius*

"If you want something new, you have to stop doing something old."
— *Peter F. Drucker*

"Intelligence is the ability to adapt to change." — *Stephen Hawking*

Given the kind of high stress environment and demanding jobs that we operate in, continuously thinking about ways to get better is inevitable. Frequently reflecting on teams' purpose is critical for long-term success. Data and trends add a lot of value to look back and discuss with some quantitative and qualitative evidence.

This section talks about a few different ways of reflecting on how teams can get better by using some basic data that can be captured everyday throughout the sprint.

- Right forecast
- Value delivery
- Milestones map
- Data center
- An avoidable fire
- Impediments map
- Dependencies map
- Retro radiator

* * *

1. RIGHT FORECAST

Situation: Ratio that is defined as the planned versus delivered items does not always work 100%. Consistently a few tasks (work items) get pushed to the next sprint regardless of good planning. There could be several reasons for this. I have listed a few of them here:

- The delay becomes a habit
- The requirements could change

However, this may not happen regularly and if it does, it is important to discuss this in the retrospective.

In case of an IT company, build errors could happen. Or the lack of a stable build could also be a reason. Sometimes, verification could take time.

If you would like the team to visualize the health of their forecast, this technique may be helpful.

This technique could be used for teams to understand how quickly they move their tasks to a completed state. They can drill down to follow where they spend most of their efforts. It helps to retrospect on how fast the teams can deliver value and discuss various factors that influence the value delivery.

Work Item	Change in scope	Build readiness	Big size	Build errors	Verification	Waiting
STORY 1						
STORY 2						
STORY 3					© Madhavi Ledalla	

Instructions

- Draw a table as shown in the image above and put it up on the whiteboard. The horizontal row represents the individual's work items and the vertical row represents the common issues that impede the team from completing their tasks as planned

- Each team member can note their work items on sticky notes and put it up on the board. You can put a check-mark in the right column for each of these tasks based on what issue is impeding their value delivery. They can update this board every day as and when tasks finish or get blocked because of issues highlighted

- At the end of this exercise we can see that the columns with the most check marks are the critical bottleneck areas

* * *

2. VALUE DELIVERY

Situation: In the beginning of the sprint, all the work items (tasks) get started. Everything was moving simultaneously, however at the end of the sprint, few items were finished. The rest of them are at 90% completion. We often come across such situations in sprints and debate what needs to be done.

One factor to inspect here is to check if the team is taking on and starting too many items in parallel. The team needs to discuss if they should start a few tasks, complete them and later start others. This technique could be used for teams to visualize when and how they start their work and drive them towards focused completion of tasks before moving on to others. This lends to the principle - "Stop Starting and Start finishing! "

Work Items	6th	7th	8th	9th	10th	13th	14th	15th	16th	17th
US-10001251	D	D	D							
US-10001353	D	D	F	T	T	TC	C			
D-10001255										
S-10001290			D	D	DC	T	C	A		
US-10001255										
US-10001451	D	D	D	D	D	D	DC	T		
D-10001255	D	DC	T	T	T					
D-10001255										
US-10001253										
US-10001255	DC	T	T	T						

© Madhavi Ledalla

The team can visualize their flow of work using a value delivery trend chart as shown above and make use of the same to retrospect their sprints. It may take an additional time of say about five minutes every day for individuals to update the table; however, the value of those five minutes will show in the end of the sprint.

The chart can be as simple as putting the days of the sprint versus the items picked up.

Legends such as

- D- Start dev
- T- Start test
- DC- Dev completed
- TC- Test completed
- A- Acceptance
- C- Complete

can be used to visualize the bottleneck area.

For example, the trend in the above picture indicates that the team is starting too many items in parallel and testing is not getting done. This could be one reason why the team is not able to complete all the forecasted work. The trend chart can include other columns to show the distinct steps in the workflow to make the underlying bottlenecks clear.

Instructions:

- Make a value delivery trend chart on the whiteboard and keep it at a place where it is easily visible and accessible to the team
- Ask the team members to update it twice every day at the start and stop of their tasks. The table is self-explanatory - each day the team needs to put down the task they are working on and update it as the work progresses
- This table gives information about some critical patterns like teams starting many tasks in parallel without completing the pending ones, the waiting time and handover trends across the different stages in their workflow
- A visual representation like this in the team's workspace gives them a constant reminder of the current work and the big picture of what exactly is going on. The team can assess if they need to start a new task or join hands to finish an existing one

* * *

3. MILESTONES MAP

Situation: A milestones map tells the story of the team's experience through the sprint from beginning to end. If you would like to see the journey of your team every day, then this technique might help you.

Ask each team member to do a milestones map identifying key events and interactions during the sprint. They need to identify important events that are worth highlighting during the retrospective. This could include client calls, meetings with the management, sales review meetings, handover and vendor management calls. Then for each of these events/interactions, they need to describe their feelings and emotions.

This journey map takes the shape of an infographic that portrays the experience of each team member regarding the important events. The X axis represents the sprint timeline and the Y axis represents the emotions on a positive or a negative scale

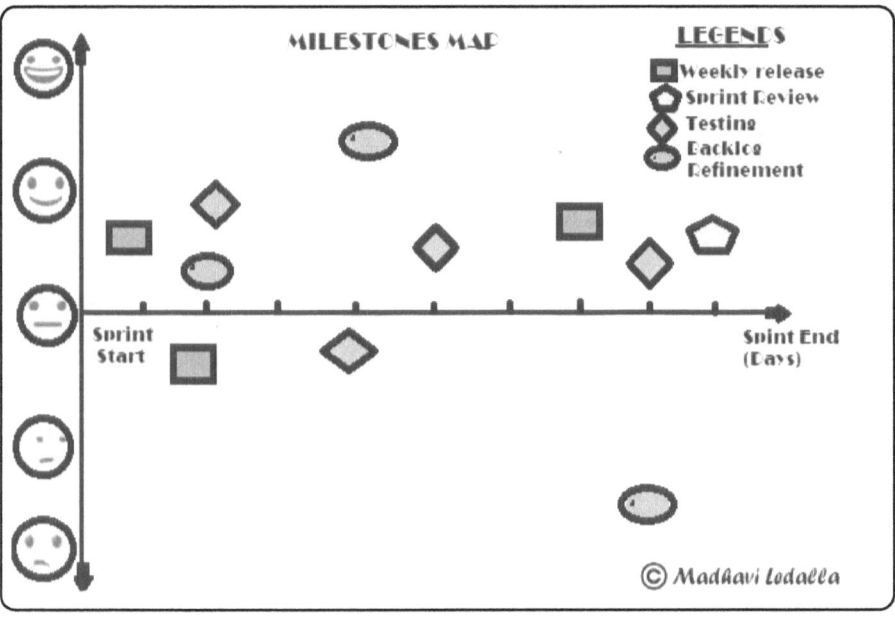

Instructions

- As a team, identify important events and interactions. Use a different colored sticky note for each event/interaction

- On a timeline from the start of the sprint to the end, depict the positive and negative emotions of each of these events/ interactions

- When the entire team completes this, you should be able to see a common pattern that emerges

- Discuss the pattern and try to understand what you can do to minimize unpleasant experiences

* * *

4. DATA CENTER

Situation: If your team likes to discuss the data that reflects the happenings of the sprint, these pointers may help. Retrospectives get more engaging and inquisitive when the discussion is backed up with team progress and delivery trends.

Instructions

Introduce the team to a few metrics as mentioned below that can be used to brainstorm their progress during the sprint:

- The progress towards the sprint goal, number of items planned versus completed
- The impediments/risks and how did the team/management huddle around these
- The teams' confidence vote on their sprint forecast after the sprint planning is done on a scale of 1 to 5 using the first of five technique. This is an excellent input for teams and managers to huddle around if the confidence is low on the sprint commitments and what can be done to improve confidence levels
- Number of backlog items planned versus accepted by the product
- Number of stories that are getting added after the sprint planning day, i.e., amount of scope being added after the sprint starts
- The cycle time (time it takes for a backlog item to move from in-progress to completed/accepted state)
- The number of days a backlog item remains in a particular state to give an indication of how fast items are moving from one stage to another
- The developer to tester handover timelines if any
- Number of defects that are being caught by the team across different environments
- The impact the developed features have on the end customers

Teams can use some of the visual radiators listed below to capture the key data trends for discussion during retrospectives

These are examples from Rally[14] which is one of the agile lifecycle management tools for agile projects.

Sprint burn down chart: This chart displays work remaining and completed in the sprint. It helps to proactively anticipate whether the committed work will be delivered by the sprint end date. It is also useful during sprint retrospective meetings to identify events during the sprint or problems with estimation during planning.

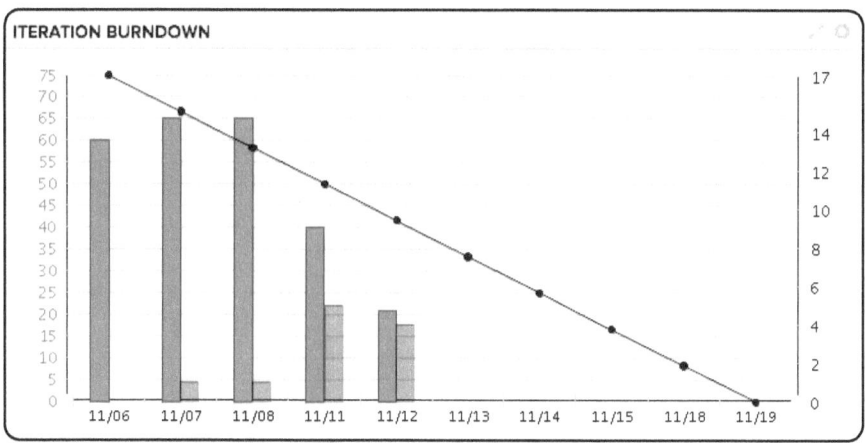

- Pending task hours are represented in blue bars
- Completed story points[15] are green bars
- Ideal burndown rate is a black line, based on the task estimate

---

[14.] https://techdocs.broadcom.com/content/broadcom/techdocs/us/en/ca-enterprise-software/agile-development-and-management/rally-platform-ca-agile-central/rally/customizing-top/use-apps/app-catalog.html
[15.] https://www.mountaingoatsoftware.com/blog/what-are-story-points

Sprint burn up chart: Displays work delivered so far in the sprint to proactively anticipate whether the sprint scope will be delivered.

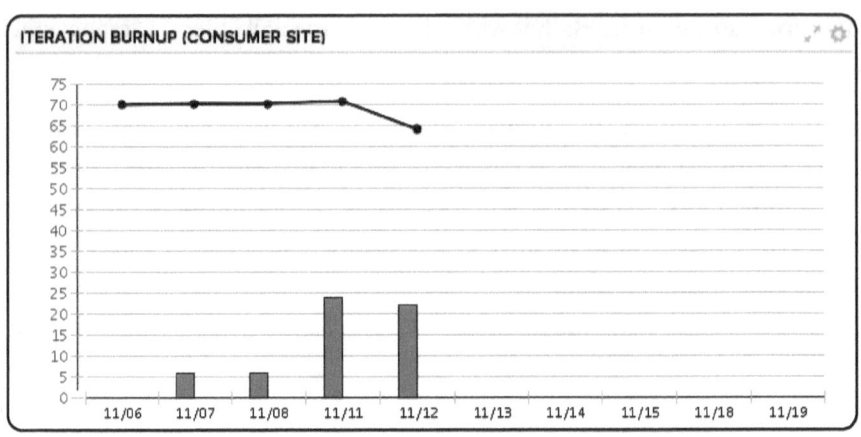

- The vertical axis represents the accepted work in hours.
- The horizontal axis represents the dates.
- Completed story points are green bars.
- Total scope of work in the sprint is a black line.

Cumulative flow: The cumulative flow diagram displays the rolled-up states of all scheduled items to help you plan and track your sprints. This diagram displays all scheduled work items for the sprint in incremental collections of days as the horizontal axis. Each day displays the rolled-up state of all scheduled items for the increment. The vertical axis of the chart portrays the total plan estimates in your specified units.

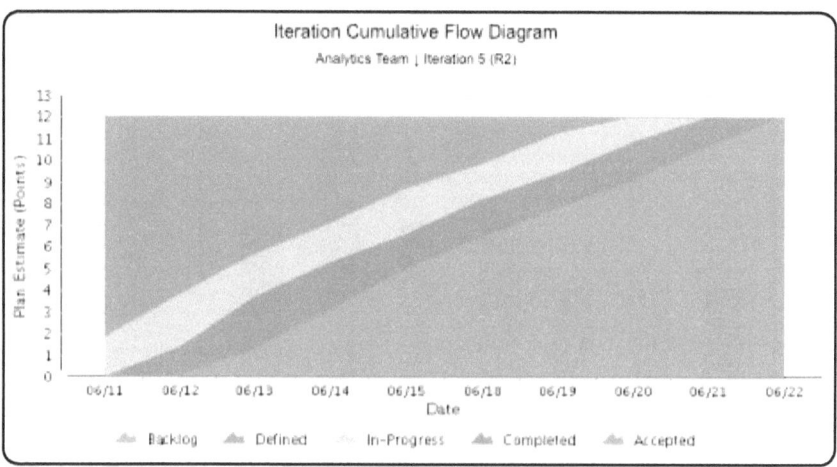

Use this diagram to:

> **Forecast and track progress:** The stages of the scheduled work items indicate the progress of your development as it moves towards completion. To determine if you are on track to complete the work within the scheduled sprint, monitor the accepted stage

> **Manage scope:** As your scheduled work item bars are at level, it is easy to see when excess work is added to a sprint. If the level of the bars does not remain uniform and instead continues to increase, you need to re-address the scope of your sprint

> **Identify bottlenecks:** Use the rolled-up stages of your scheduled work items to determine if there are trends that indicate bottlenecks. For example, a large section of scheduled items in a completed stage as compared to a small amount of accepted may indicate a testing roadblock

Sprint defects by priority: The defects by priority chart provides at-a-glance view of all defects in the selected sprint, that are categorized by priority and with any state value other than closed. Use this chart to help you quickly track and recognize the number of defects of greatest importance and to ensure defect resolution is progressing in line with the sprint timeline. This chart helps to verify that the most important defects are resolved first.

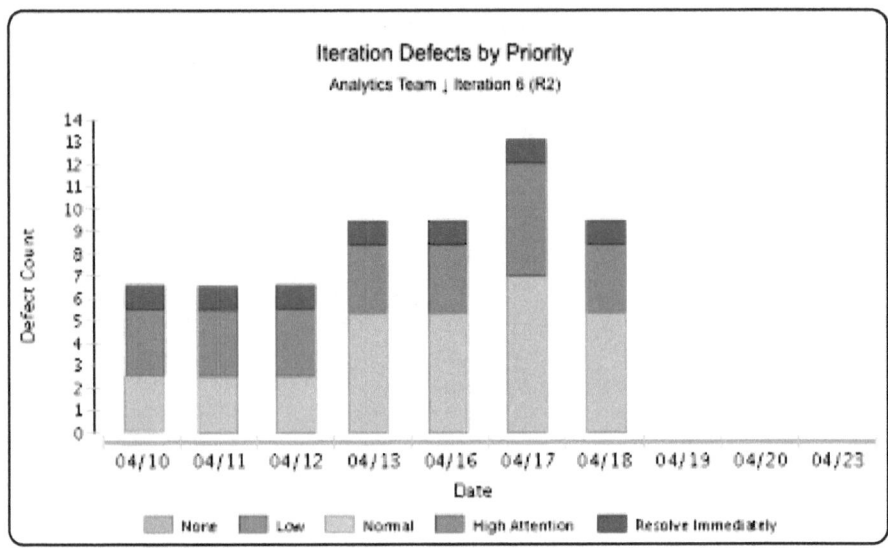

Velocity chart: The velocity chart displays all accepted plan estimate units for each of the last 10 completed sprints. Use this chart to determine your sprint velocity across projects within scope in the current workspace.

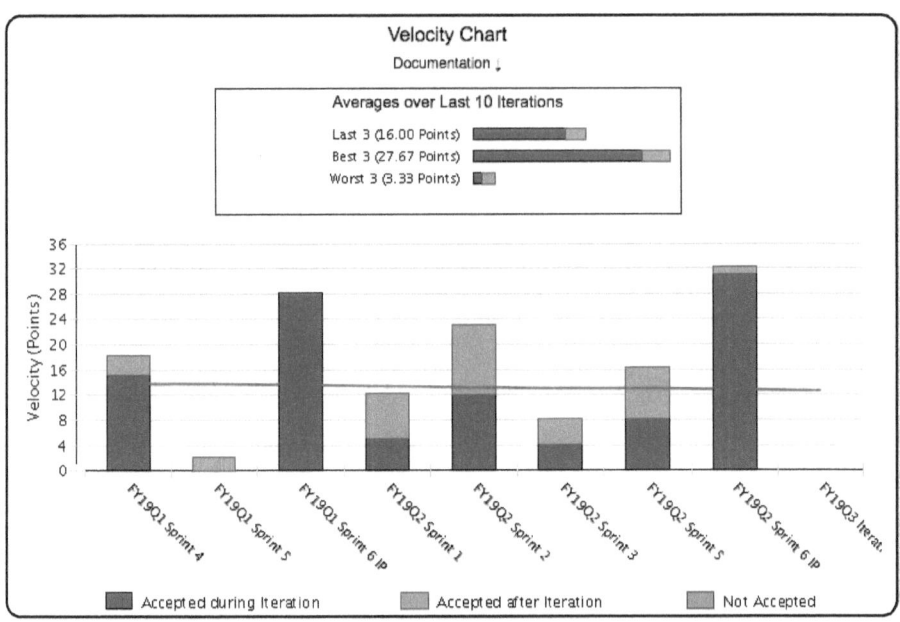

Release burn up chart: A burn up chart tracks how much work is done. The burn up chart can show more information than a burn down chart because it also has a line showing how much work is in the project as whole (the scope as workload) and this can change. The burn up chart displays work delivered so far in the release to predict whether the release date will be met.

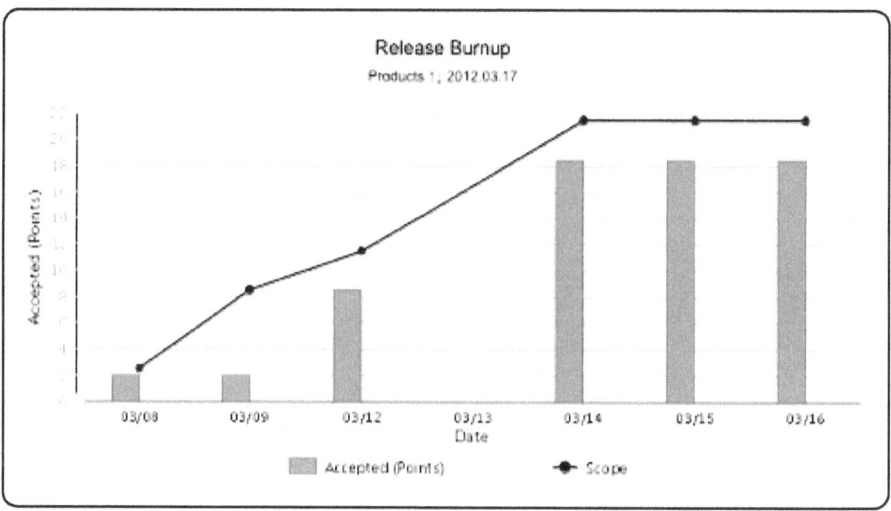

Scope change: This widget displays all work items (user stories, defects and defect suites) that have been added or removed from sprint, this gives a succinct view of whether the scope is changing during the course of sprint.

```
Iteration Scope Change

Iteration      FY19 Sprint 8    08/22/2018 - 09/04/2018

Show Work   ● All   ○ Added   ○ Removed

                    Count    Points
  + Total Added       5       0.0
  - Total Removed     2       0.0
    Net               3       0.0
```

The portfolio item timeline: This widget allows you to visualize how portfolio items are progressing over varying time intervals. Portfolio managers, product managers, and other executives can use the app to quickly see if a portfolio item is ahead of schedule, in danger, or behind schedule compared to the planned start and end dates. Actual progress bars are colored for quick reference to status.

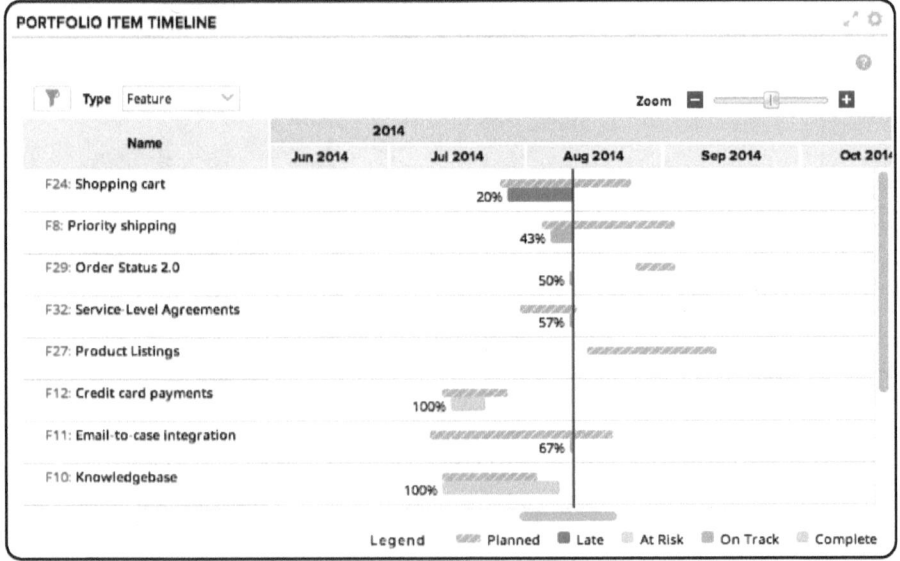

This data driven approach is an example of using an inside-out approach i.e., creating a structure that will help inculcate a culture of collaboration and self-organization among teams including the leaders by using very basic vital information visible and transparent for inspecting, and adapting the trend.

Once the discussion is done using some of these visual radiators, teams could set objective goals like 5% increase in a specific area and come up with an action plan for getting there.

(Reference: Rally Central Help)

* * *

5. AN AVOIDABLE FIRE

Situation: Do you see your team taking shortcuts to fixing a problem instead of getting to resolving the issues from the root? This exercise will help your team understand the value of finding the right solutions to a problem instead of seeking an easier way out.

All of us know that when the problem is small, it is better to address it and fix it then and there. However, sometimes we ignore such issues.

I was once on a camping trip with my friends and we were enjoying our evening around a bonfire. Suddenly, the direction of the wind changed and a few books that were kept around were engulfed in the fire, we extinguished the fire on the books and continued to chat. In a short while, the wind currents became stronger and the fire from the bonfire spread to the tent. We had to rush out of the spot immediately. Had we planned well when the breeze was light, we could have avoided the bigger mess.

When I was working with one of my teams, I could connect this experience with what the team was going through. They were ignoring the actual problem in their tasks and were trying to patch it up temporarily instead of solving it permanently owing to lack of time and delivery pressure. I have seen such unattended problems surface during the time of delivery when the team needed to slog to fix the problem from the root.

I wanted the team to retrospect and think hard about what happens if they take short cuts while working on a few issues. I also wanted them to analyze the time they needed to fix the real issue.

Instructions

- Print (or draw) the above picture and put it up on the whiteboard. Distribute marker pens and sticky notes
- Explain the context to the team and ask them to think about the issues they face during their sprints
- List down the implications of not fixing them
- Ask them to discuss the actions required to fix the issues

* * *

6. IMPEDIMENTS MAP

Situation: If you would like to help your teams visualize impediments that they come across during sprints, this may help.

Impediment	Date Logged	Date Resolved	Age	Impact
				© Madhavi Ledalla

Instructions

Ask your team to use a visual radiator for logging impediments that the team comes through during their sprints. The age of the impediment shows how long the impediment was alive. This board needs to be updated by the team daily during the sprint to indicate the number of impediments and their impact on the sprint goal including the resolution time.

This board can also include the levels of escalations for the impediment to be scaled up to the next level of leadership in case the impediment does not get resolved in the given duration as shown below:

Impediment Name	Date Logged	Date Resolved	Age	Resolution
Age > 5 days	Point of Escalation	Date Resolved	Age	Resolution
Age > 10 days	Point of Escalation	Date Resolved	Age	Resolution
				© Madhavi Ledalla

***

7. DEPENDENCIES MAP

Situation: If you want your team to think about the number of dependencies that it comes across during sprints and if that is the reason why the team is not able to meet the sprint goal, then this may be a technique that might help.

Dependency	Work Item	Date Identified	Impact	Date Resolved	Reason for Dependency
					© Madhavi Ledalla

Instructions

Ask the team to prepare this table during their sprint, and keep updating every day during the sprint or as and when they get some blocker. Review this data during retrospectives - this gives some very useful insights around the reason for dependencies that may include the team structure, cross-functional capabilities, inter-team priority issues or dependency on external team members. The discussions using such evidence may help the team to think through how they can overcome similar bottlenecks in the future. If we don't manage the dependencies well, dependencies will soon start managing us.

This data may also give some very good insights to the leadership team about critical issues that impede the team from delivering from a structural and process perspective.

* * *

8. RETRO RADIATOR

Situation: If you are looking for a visual radiator that would help the team keep track of action items discovered in the sprints and the consequent progress made on these items, then this board will be useful. This could be a single point reference for all action items identified during retrospectives. Keeping this radiator at a place that is visible to the team adds value as it helps the team to reflect on the action items whenever they look at the board.

Sprint	To-Do	In-Progress	Done	Waiting
1			▢▢▢	▢
2	▢	▢	▢▢	
3	▢		▢▢▢	▢
4	▢▢▢	▢		

© Madhavi Ledalla

Many times, we tend to forget action items that are derived from a retrospective. However, it is important to follow-up on action items that the team identifies in retrospectives. Before starting a retrospective, revisiting the previous retrospective's action items and checking status is an imperative step.

To keep this process going, tracking the action items needs its own process. Having a visual indicator of the action items, along with the people responsible for them, always helps the team stay focused. Tracking can be done in different ways. We can use an electronic tool or a visual indicator as shown in the figure above.

Instructions

- Draw the retro radiator classification table, with the following columns – Sprint, To Do, In Progress, Done, Waiting.

- For each actionable item, place them under one of the 5 categories. The meaning of the classification is as follows:

    - *Sprint:* In which sprint were the action items identified
    - *To Do:* Action items yet to be worked on
    - *In Progress:* Action items being worked on
    - *Done:* Completed action items
    - *Waiting:* Action items that are waiting on something else to support their getting done

- On each card, write the name of the owner responsible for the execution of that item.

PART SIX

Going Beyond The Routine

GOING BEYOND THE ROUTINE

CHAPTER 09

"The only way to discover the limits of the possible is to go beyond them into the impossible." – Arthur C. Clarke

"Innovation is seeing what everybody has seen and thinking what nobody has thought." – Dr. Albert Szent-Györgyi

"Anything's possible if you've got enough nerve." – J.K. Rowling

Innovation and creativity are part of everyone's work. Sometimes teams get stuck in monotonous work and get into a routine. They lose the groove of getting creative and enjoying the normal routine. Tiny drops of water make a mighty ocean. Innovation does not mean they have to create something big or different – it can start from everyday life. What can we do differently within the existing constraints? These frameworks will help you think in that direction.

- Team Yaan
- Set me free
- Up cycle
- Foresee the future
- Delay cost balloon
- Tasty cake

***

1. TEAM YAAN

Situation: For particularly critical and high-visibility projects, every error is presented in front of thousands of eyes. This activity is specifically meant for critical projects. This metaphorical activity helps teams understand enablers and impediments and especially works well while the project is nearing completion.

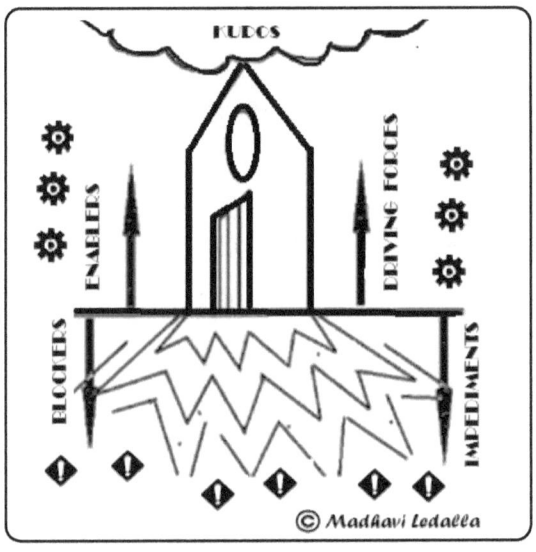

Mangalyaan (Mars Orbiter Mission) was India's first interplanetary project, which was launched in 2013. The launch of this space probe was a big event. Any critical, high visibility project is no less than launching a spacecraft!

When India sent Mangalyaan to space, one of my teams had a retrospective scheduled for the next day. So, I thought I could relate better to the team by using Mangalyaan's launch! We drew a picture of a rocket on the board and named it "Team Yaan". We noted that while Mangalyaan has one year to reach its target, our project had just one sprint left to complete its release. It was the most critical, high-visibility project in the organization, as important as the Mangalyaan was for India.

I said, "As a team, let us identify the driving forces - i.e., what we need to keep doing to ensure that we hit the target - as well as the pulling forces - the impediments and bottlenecks that are keeping us from reaching the target."

The use of a piece of news, which was fresh in everyone's minds, helped that retrospective well. The team was excited, and they came up with great insights to move forward.

Instructions

- Print the above picture (or draw it) and put it up on the whiteboard
- Explain the context and ask the team to compare their project to the launch of spacecraft. Ask them to visualize using the picture on the whiteboard
- Encourage the team to identify enablers or driving forces that have kept the project on track so far
- Identify blockers or pulling forces that will put the project at risk
- Arrive at ways to protect your project from the blockers

* * *

2. SET ME FREE

Situation: Often teams have constraints owing to which they do not move forward. If you want your work to be free from constraints they face, this may be the technique that will work.

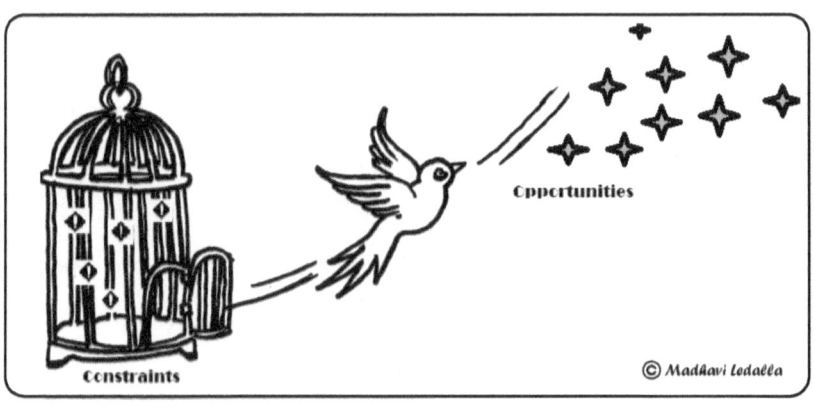

Sometimes, teams work across countries and continents. All individuals cannot travel across the globe to meet everyone in their team. This lack of personal interaction could be a constraint that is placing a roadblock for collaboration. How can you convert these constraints into opportunities?

In one of my retrospective meetings, I described the situation of a bird that is confined to a cage and asked the team what could be done to let the bird explore the world. "Set it free! Let it fly," came the prompt response.

I used that response and asked the team, "Do we think our team also has similar constraints because of which we cannot explore the limitless possibilities in front of us?" For a moment the team was silent, but they slowly opened up. This was an *'aha'* moment for me and I understood how well the team could relate to setting a bird free.

I repeatedly say that certain occurrences around us could connect to the team in their retrospectives. This method is especially useful for teams and leadership to debate on constraints they face and ways to convert these into opportunities.

Instructions

- Draw the picture above (or print it out) on the whiteboard

- Describe the constraints the bird feels in a cage, ask the team how it feels when it is set free

- Ask the team to think of constraints they face in their teams that are limiting them from exploring the world of opportunities. Ask them to write them down on sticky notes and put it inside the cage

- Ask them about the opportunities they see in front of them that they would like to leverage if set free from the constraints. Write these down on sticky notes and put it outside the cage

- Encourage the team to think through the limitations and provide the leadership an insight into the constraints and how leadership support could help the team explore the world of possibilities

- As part of this discussion, you could also ask team members to think about what they can do on their own to overcome a few of these constraints by themselves. In effect, this exercise helps the team arrive at what is their scope of control

* * *

3. UP CYCLE

Situation: Your teams may often get stuck in daily tasks and repetitive work. It is a good practice to break the routine once in a while and re-energize the team to give them a fresh perspective of looking at things. Do you wish to break this monotony and try something new? This exercise will work best!

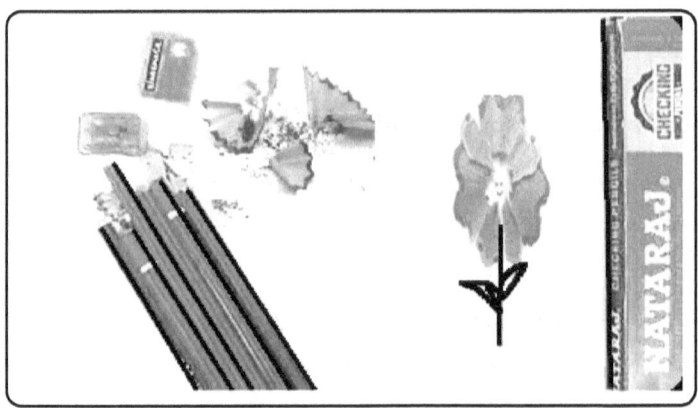

To me innovation is not always about creating something new out of the blue. It is about identifying a method of doing the existing work differently for a better outcome or to try something new to support experiential learning.

Having said that, it is not an easy job to motivate your team to innovate amidst the regular delivery pressures. This metaphor was born when I was contemplating ways of facilitating a discussion around innovation with my team.

I was waiting for my dear daughter at her arts class, there I saw a few children who were sharpening their pencils. They saved the pencil shavings in a little box. A little while later, they used these shavings to decorate a card they were making. I could connect the children's experience to the concept of innovation. They used the existing resources to come up with something valuable and new. And, I used this thought to facilitate a discussion with my team.

Going Beyond the Routine • 157

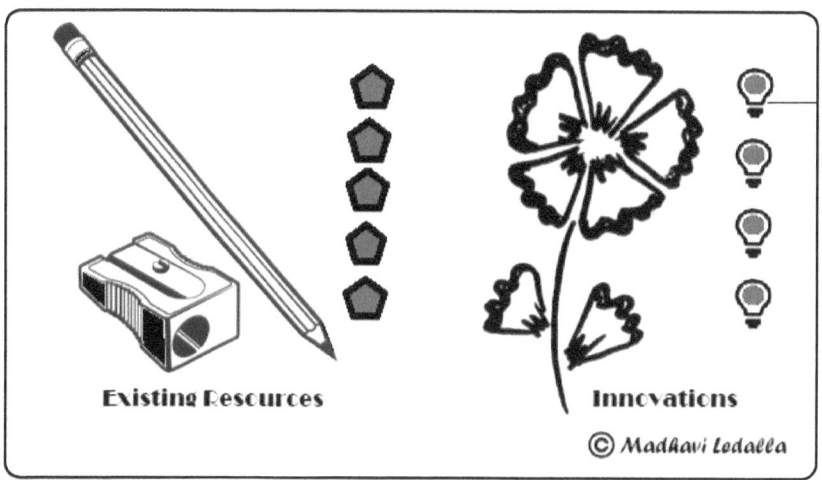

Instructions

▶ Put up the above picture on a whiteboard. Distribute sticky notes and markers

▶ Explain the metaphor to the team. Assume that the pencil and sharpener are the resources at their disposal. Encourage them to think of ways in which they can do things differently in their everyday work

▶ Put up the list of existing resources on the pencil/sharpener section on the board

▶ Put up the list of new innovations along the other side of the board that the team wishes to try using the available resources.

Remember, creativity and innovation do not mean inventing something new or big. It is as simple as finding a different or an efficient way of doing the same existing work.

* * *

4. FORESEE THE FUTURE

Situation: None of us are fortune tellers and we do not know what the future holds for us. However, retrospectives can also be used to understand how teams wish to visualize their future. Here is an example of how you could engage your team to visualize their future state.

Imagine you now have laid the foundation to your house and in the future plan to build a beautiful big mansion. You make the blueprint and start planning the construction. You foresee what it will look like in three months, six months and a year. You might also plan for two years.

You can use this metaphor to plan a sprint or release retrospective too.

Instructions
- Put up the picture above on the whiteboard. Distribute markers and sticky notes
- Ask the team to describe their current state of work and capture it on the left. The current state can be related to the ongoing release trends or could be about any aspect the team wishes to discuss and debate upon
- Then ask them to visualize how they would like to envision their future state. Capture the thoughts on the right side
- Then ask them what they want to do if they would like to move from current to their wish list of ideal state

* * *

5. DELAY COST BALLOON

Situation: Does your team often miss their forecast, and end up paying a price for it? This exercise will help you discuss the issue within the team and help them reflect on the reasons.

I was once planning to attend a conference but had not made up my mind about it. Falsely assuming I had more time, I missed the window for the early bird discount and had to pay double the amount for the tickets when I finally got them. I incurred an additional expense of $ 100!

Often, people do this in many situations. They delay a few tasks and end up incurring additional expense. One of the teams I worked with constantly missed their forecast and were paying the price - additional expense, extra effort and an impact on the overall release schedule.

In their team retrospective, I shared my conference ticket example and used a balloon metaphor to describe the scenario. The more air you pump into the balloon, the more it inflates. Imagine the balloon as your delay store - the more you delay, the more delay cost you incur. Over time the size of the balloon gets to a substantial proportion if you don't take corrective or preventive measures.

In the team retrospectives, I asked each of the team members to draw their balloons on the board, the size of the balloon being proportional to the amount of work not done according to plan. Everyone drew their own balloons of different sizes. Following this, I asked them to think and write the impact on sticky notes and put it inside the balloon.

Then I asked the team what they can do so that the balloon size decreases at least in the next sprint and attach these ideas as strings to the balloon.

Instructions
- Put up the above picture on the whiteboard. Distribute markers and sticky notes
- Explain the balloon metaphor and ask them to imagine blowing air into a balloon equivalent to the undone work that is pushed to the next sprint
- Ask them to think about how the size of the balloon grows proportional to the amount of air blown
- Encourage them to assess the cost of delay i.e., the impact, write them down on sticky notes and put it inside the balloon
- Once you have all balloons ask the team to reflect and discuss each other's balloons
- Discuss what could be done to avoid this situation in the future and put up these suggestions as strings to the balloon

* * *

6. TASTY CAKE

Situation: Does your team perform several activities, a lot of which are repetitive or do not add value? Do you want to optimize your team's effort by eliminating redundant activities? This technique will help address such a situation and make your team productive in a short span of time.

This method helps teams assess how much non-value-added work they are incurring into as debt sprint over a sprint. It is handy for teams to assess their value delivery efficiency.

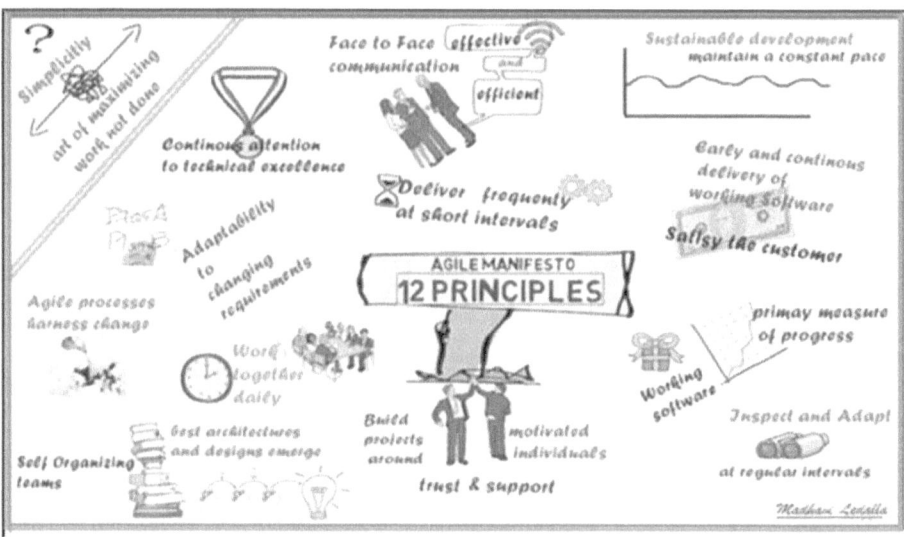

Once, while I was by myself, I was pondering over the 12 principles behind the agile Manifesto. One principle is, "Simplicity - the art of maximizing the amount of work not done - is essential." I mulled over why this principle is called an art, while others are not? And why should we maximize the amount of work not done?

The answer to this came to me when I worked on the agile transformation for an organization. While working on this transformation, I focused on a few key aspects – I picked up only a certain number of tasks that were doable in a sprint and focused on implementing the essential design that supports functionality. We worked hard to keep things simple and kept looking for tasks that did not add value – reducing such activities.

As I continued my journey, I learnt to implement this principle in many everyday tasks. I have learnt why practicing this principle is an "art", and mastering this art is the key. This agile principle lends itself to one of the key elements of lean – eliminating waste. By maximizing the work not done, a continuous value flow can be achieved by optimizing the value delivery chain.

The best way of interpreting this principle in your daily work is to ask a question every time you decide: "Am I adding value by doing this?" The goal is to deliver the highest value with the fewest number of items.

I have used this "art" as a trigger point in sprint retrospectives to deliver utmost value!

Instructions

▷ Print the above picture and put it up on the whiteboard. Introduce the team to the concept of the agile principle – Simplicity, the art of maximizing work not done is essential. Use the cake ordering metaphor in the above picture to discuss the principle

➤ Ask the team to discuss what types of activities they think can be optimized to lead towards productive and positive outcomes quickly

➤ Ask them to discuss activities that do not add value and the ones that can be eliminated

You can also take the example of a Microsoft Word and ask them how many features it has? It has around 100 features. Then, ask the team how many of these features do we use. Tell your team that the art of maximizing the amount of work not done lies in identifying the tasks which have no value-adds so that one can get to the most important items.

PART SEVEN

Personal Reflection

CHAPTER 10

PERSONAL REFLECTION

"Each of us has an undeniable responsibility to ourselves and the rest of the world to be our personal best on any given day."
— *Laurie Buchanan*

"Life is not a competition with others. Life is a competition with yourself – to do your personal best each day." — *Cameron C. Taylor*

The focus of this section is to create a lightweight environment where people can open and talk about their values, feelings and perceptions and how they see themselves in the context of the bigger team or how the team sees them in context of the organization.

➢ Three monkeys

➢ The best "you"

➢ Value tree

➢ Model your sprint

➢ Picture your sprint

➢ The chemical reaction

* * *

1. THREE MONKEYS

Situation: This exercise is very helpful in the case of one-on-one retrospectives, where individuals can express how they wish the next sprint would be for them. It helps them understand and offer feedback on their experience in the team at large.

This technique could also be used for the teams to help them arrive at how differently they could work on the next sprint.

Everyone knows about the 'Three Wise Monkeys'! This is a pictorial maxim, embodying the proverbial principle «see no evil, hear no evil, speak no evil». The three monkeys are Mizaru, covering his eyes, who sees no evil; Kikazaru, covering his ears, who hears no evil; and Iwazaru, covering his mouth, who speaks no evil.

I have a little sculpture representing the 'Three Wise Monkeys' at home. As I looked at it, it struck me that I could use them during one of my team retrospectives. In the next retrospective, I asked the team to think about what they would like to see in their next sprint, what they would like to hear in their next sprint and what they would like to speak in their next sprint

This story connected very well with the team, and it helped them arrive at how they would like their next sprint to be.

Personal Reflection • 169

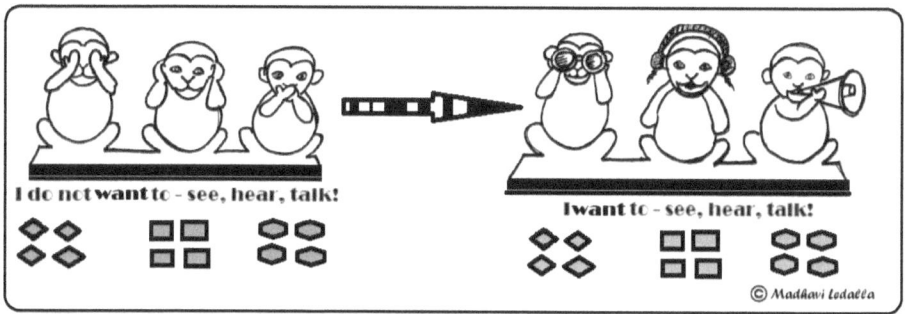

Instructions

- Print the above picture (or draw it) and put it up on the whiteboard
- Explain the context to the team and ask them to visualize using the picture
- Ask the team about what they would like to see in their next sprint, what they would like to hear in their next sprint and what they would like to speak in their next sprint
- To add more data, you could also ask the team to think about what they do not want to see, hear and speak in their next sprint. Then ask them to collaboratively discuss what they can do so that their "Do not want" wish list does not come true!

✳ ✳ ✳

2. THE BEST "YOU"

Situation: After completing multiple sprints and conducting several retrospectives, teams often believe that there is nothing to retrospect as everything is moving smoothly. This is the time to question them about what would make them go from good to great.

This activity helps the team move ahead after they have reached a comfortable dynamic level where everything works well.

Discuss with team about what they think are characteristics of a high-performing team. Ask them what it means to them and ask them to define a criterion for the same. Encourage the team to ask themselves if they are high performing. Ask them to come up with areas of improvement to help them reach this stage.

This exercise could also be useful in a school or an educational institution. Children from a particular school perform well at the school level tests, however, the performance dips when they face a national level test. "Good to Great" will help you drill down to the root cause of this problem.

When I worked with a team using this exercise, several interesting discussions surfaced. This team was performing well and could finish the work during the sprints consistently. However, their work was going to the production stage only at the end of every quarter. Although the development pipeline was agile, the release pipeline was not. While as a team they did their job well, they realized that they needed to improve their technical practices that would reduce their release timelines. So, the team pondered on what they could do to speed up the release pipeline.

There are several such instances where the team is doing well, however, when looked at from a system thinking perspective, scope for improvement may emerge.

Instructions

- Ask teams how they feel about their sprints. Ask them to elaborate on what is going well. Ask them to put these down in the "Good" section

- Then ask them what they need to do so they become a great team. Put these thoughts down in the "Great" section

- Generate discussions on different topics. If you are an IT company, your discussion could involve zero-defects, automation, zero-build errors, no memory leaks, escaped defects count, daily builds and daily check-ins

- Explore other areas of improvement that could push the team to become a high-performance team

***

3. VALUE TREE

Situation: All of us have certain values that define our identity and drive our behavior. However sometimes the discrepancy between self-perception and reality gets us into trouble. If you would like to brainstorm on your personal values and ways to back them up with our actions, this exercise will get everyone on the team to the point.

One day I was casually talking with my team and observed that one of my team members wasn't happy as she had to sacrifice some of her values to adapt herself to the new team. She was always keen about delivering quality, even if a timely fix did not go to the client. The team was under pressure to ensure the client received responses quickly, even if it was temporary. Hence she had to do certain activities like compromising on testing cycles and had to let go some of her personal values to meet the team commitments. I had a conversation with her and discussed what other options she had and finally we picked a few options so that the similar situations can be avoided in the future.

The 'value tree' is a good way to reach out to your team to discuss their personal values and to understand how to fit them with the rest of the team. It shows the distinction between the individual values and the team values, and the overlap between them.

Instructions

- Put up the picture above on the whiteboard. Distribute markers and sticky notes

- Use green sticky notes to list personal values that the individuals feel are satisfied within the team

- Use brown sticky notes to list personal values that are not being met by being part of the team

- You can also use red sticky notes to list the values that are the weakest links in the team

- Discuss the values in brown and red, and understand how to move them to green

* * *

4. MODEL YOUR SPRINT

Situation: Sometimes teams need a break from writing and sitting down. If your team is ready for some physical activity, this exercise will be the perfect fit. I often use "play dough" during my trainings for simulating sprints and helping them run the end-to-end sequence of events. Play dough works well with my training delivery model as it encourages participants to come up with their own ideas and build a product they would like to see.

I have been experimenting with it for retrospectives, and it works well here too. This exercise fosters collaborative group discussions that are fun and engaging. It gives them a break from their regular work, while making them work with their hands to depict their journey together.

Instructions

- Handover play dough set to team and ask them to come up with a model that is a depiction of their understanding of the last sprint including their feelings and thoughts

- Give the team five minutes to first come up with a model design and then give 15 minutes to build the same using play dough. Discuss the final model

You can execute this game in two ways:

- Variant 1: Ask the entire team to build one model and talk about their sprint journey

- Variant 2: Ask individual team members to come up with their own models to represent their emotions related to the sprint. After completion, each team member can share their model and what changes they would like to see in it so it represents their ideal sprint (i.e. future state)

You can collate all discussions and actionable items into a to-do list for their ideal sprint.

* * *

5. PICTURE YOUR SPRINT

Situation: Does your team like to get creative and draw their thoughts? This exercise will help you work with their creativity.

While the exercise gives creative space for the team to express their emotions regarding the sprint, it also helps the team collaborate with each other. It gives them room to talk to one another and learn about how the sprint felt for everyone.

Instructions

- Ask the team to get creative and picture their sprint using cartoons, proverbs or in any other way in their drawing
- Ask them to describe their artwork

You can execute this game in two ways:

- Variant 1: Ask the entire team to create one artwork that talks about their collective sprint journey

➤ Variant 2: Ask individual team members to come up with their own artworks to represent their sprint. After completion, each team member can share their artwork and what changes they would like to see in it so it represents their ideal sprint (i.e. future state)

You can collate all discussions and actionable items into a to-do list for their ideal sprint.

❋ ❋ ❋

6. THE CHEMICAL REACTION

Situation: If you would like to share with your teammates or reflect by yourself on what motivates you to aim for higher and keep going, then this may be an interesting exercise for you.

I have always had a habit of writing down a few articles, but never had the confidence to post it online for multiple reasons. On one fine day, after I posted my first article on retrospectives 'Knock on wood' on Scrum Alliance website, I received positive feedback and likes from the readers. This feedback motivated me to write more and I started my blogging journey. So, I believe every endeavor will have some catalyst that will lead to the next bigger steps.

One day I was waiting outside a lab at my child's school and was watching students doing experiments in the chemistry lab. I was seeing how when adding different chemicals, they were acting as catalysts to initiate the reaction. It was a very natural process that when there are some catalyzing elements the reaction follows. I related this to how the feedback and responses I got from my readers helped me continue my blogging journey.

There will be many such situations in your personal life, you may have a goal to achieve, and you just need those chemicals/catalysts that will help you meet your targets. In my case, the catalysts were a place where readers could access my article and give feedback. So, if anyone would like to reflect on their goals and what catalysts would help them meet their goals, and how they can work towards making these catalysts a reality then you can use this metaphor.

Instructions

- Draw the picture above or take a print out and place on a white board
- Goal: Write down what you would like to achieve i.e., your goal. Put that one big goal inside the flask
- Catalysts: Add chemicals that you think will cause the reaction and turn the aim into reality, and put these outside the flask
- Enablers: Next think about what you can do from your side to cause the reaction and add those items to the hands of the flask!

For example, one of the goals could be picking up a different career line when you are in mid-career transition period.

- For example, a goal could be that you would like to become a content writer
- The catalysts could be people should be able to see you as a seasoned writer, like your posts and reach out to you for work
- The way you could achieve this i.e., the enablers could be doing a quick course, choose your customer segment, decide what to write, start publishing on Word Press, tweet the same on Twitter, share insights on Instagram, Facebook and other social media platforms so that you are reaching a wider set of audience. Ensure that you write on relevant topics that are of interest to your target audience

PART EIGHT

Address The State of Mind

ADDRESS THE STATE OF MIND

CHAPTER 11

"If your emotional abilities aren't in hand, if you don't have self-awareness, if you are not able to manage your distressing emotions, if you can't have empathy and have effective relationships, then no matter how smart you are, you are not going to get very far." – Daniel Goleman

"One aspect of a successful relationship is not just how compatible you are, but how you deal with your incompatibility." – Daniel Goleman

"The only way to change someone's mind is to connect with them from the heart." – Rasheed Ogunlaru

These set of frameworks are meant to tap into the emotional well-being of an individual or a team. They help you explore the unspoken thoughts and feelings of individuals, and team members so that we can understand their inner beliefs, thoughts and struggles. We all know that only when team members are happy and content from within then the outer self will be able to perform well and deliver great products.

The frameworks in this section will help you travel through emotions, stress levels and personal values that signify how much a person or team is self-content from inside and is at peace.

Following frameworks are discussed in this section:

- Pulse check
- The balance
- Safe space
- Positive sandbox
- Roundtable
- Dream catcher
- Balanced sandbox

✳ ✳ ✳

1. PULSE CHECK

Situation: Sometimes you may sense that your team is being stressed out and anxious. In such a situation, you might want to read the pulse of your team to understand their feelings and emotions. This activity will help you discuss with your team on how they felt about their sprint journey.

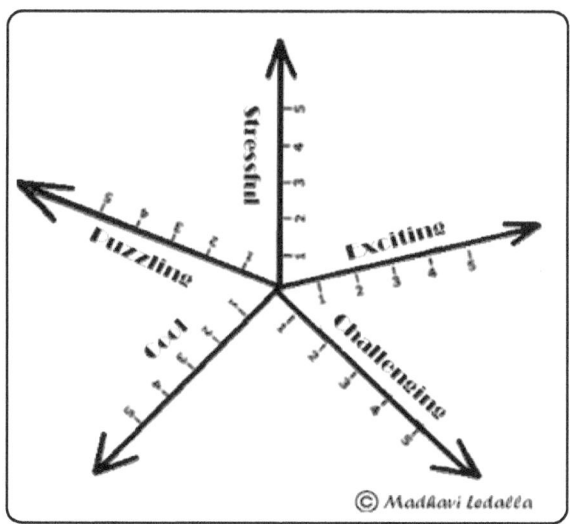

During the sprint, a few members of the team might feel concerned and worried, while others might feel exhausted or happy. And these feelings may not come out naturally if we just ask them – "Hey! Tell me how you feel about the last sprint!" As feelings are hard to quantify, when asked people often respond in binaries of good or bad.

Instead, if you create a space using a few parameters and use a scale of evaluation, you can build room for discussion. These parameters help to get a holistic view about the team's feelings and emotions. The picture shown above can be customized depending on the parameters that you want to assess your team.

This exercise will help understand and validate every individual's experience, perception, and emotions in the sprint, while giving an opportunity for further introspection. This might help move the team to a positive frame of mind instead of focusing on the downside.

Instructions

- Draw the picture above (or print it out) on the whiteboard
- Hand out a sticky note and a marker to each team member
- Give each member five minutes to introspect about the last sprint and assess how they felt in that period
- Ask them to put down a rating for each of the parameters on their sticky note, and one by one come up to the board and pin it on the appropriate axis. They could choose any or all of the five emotions specified on the board
- Ask them to explain their rating as they put it up and discuss it with everyone

* * *

2. THE BALANCE

Situation: Sometimes the team is stuck in a tight spot since they have to balance too many things. Quantity vs quality, sales targets vs customer service targets or employee satisfaction vs client satisfaction - these are some of the issues that you have to balance in everyday work. Do you want your team to be able to handle these issues and balance their outcomes better? This exercise will suit your purpose perfectly.

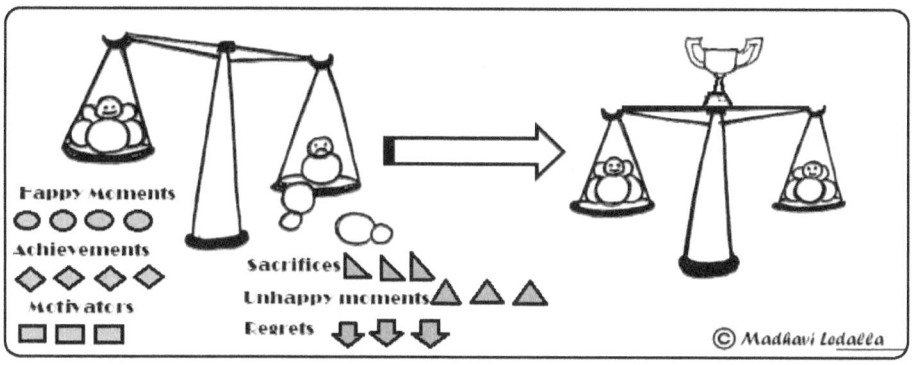

Once while buying vegetables from the local market, I saw the seller balance the vegetables on one hand and the scale on the other. Although this is a common event for me, on that day it looked different. I was reminded of how all of us are always up to a balancing act. We balance several things at work along with our personal values/commitments. I can recall many instances when I had to balance between my career progression and my family, and I had to let go of a few ambitions at work a few times.

Similarly, teams often try to balance between delivery and quality, scope and capacity or testing and development. It gets tough to define which decision is right and what is wrong in such situations.

During a team retrospective when the team was struggling with a similar balancing act, this exercise proved to be of great help in moving towards a resolution.

I drew the image of a balance on the board and placed the team goal right on top. On the left scale of the balance, I marked tasks that were going according to plan to meet the goal. On the right scale, I noted tasks that were falling behind the planned schedule. I asked my team to question what they could do together to move from a state of imbalance to a state of balance.

This works well for personal retrospectives as well. For example, when I used this exercise with an HR team, their goal was to meet the target of recruiting 100 people in three months. To accomplish this, they had to balance a few factors like quality of candidates, weekend working and overhead charges to the recruiting outsourcing contractor as the need was urgent. However, they were also happy about achieving the goal and the positive factors they listed included collaboration and leadership support. When asked how they wished to operate if they had to meet a similar goal again, there were several interesting ideas that came up. Some of them were having more cross-functional teams with a pipeline of trusted vendors and maintaining a database of rejected candidates, potential rehires for future etc.

Instructions

- Put up the picture above on the whiteboard. Distribute markers and sticky notes
- Explain the concept of this exercise and encourage the team to come up with tasks that are out of balance on the scales
- Discuss ways to balance the scales and list out potential solutions

* * *

3. SAFE SPACE

Situation: Sometimes you may see that the team is hesitant to bring up discussion points. If you see that the team shies away from opening up or they hesitate to attend meetings, this technique is very helpful.

However, the preferred alternative is to have a one-to-one conversation and address their apprehensions.

This technique helps when people are initially reluctant to speak out when the team is in the brainstorming phase. Create a ballot box and keep it in the team space along with some sticky notes. The team can use the sticky notes and put down their thoughts regarding their sprint into the ballot box, as and when it comes up. This way, they won't forget anything.

However, this is not a permanent solution. Over a period of time, you should stop using the ballot box as every team member should be comfortable speaking openly during retrospectives. The team needs to know that if an issue needs immediate attention, they should bring it up right away instead of waiting until the retrospective.

Instructions

- Make a ballot box, and place green and red colored sticky notes along with pens
- Give instructions to the team that whenever they have any thought or comment related to the sprint, they can write them on the sticky notes and put them in the box
- The green sticky notes are to indicate what is positive in the sprint and the red sticky notes indicate impediments or issues
- Open the box during the retrospective and discuss

* * *

4. POSITIVE SANDBOX

Situation: This technique helps in understanding the behavior from a neuroscience perspective. If you are a leader who would like to promote a culture that makes the team feel empowered instead of threatened then this concept will be of interest to you.

> *"In a world of increasing interconnectedness and rapid change, there is a growing need to improve the way people work together. Understanding the true drivers of human social behavior is becoming ever more urgent in this environment."* – David Rock[16]

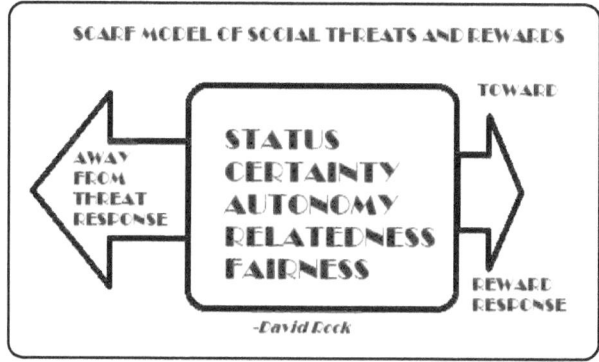

Agile talks about empowering teams so that they can self-organize around sprint goals and take ownership of deliverables. The SCARF model talks about the concept of minimizing threats and maximizing rewards so that individuals stay secure amid changing dynamics and take risks to experiment and learn.

David Rock created the SCARF model (https://www.cleverism.com/scarf-model-influence-people/) based on neuroscience research. This model describes the five domains - status, certainty, autonomy, relatedness and fairness that influence people's behavior in social situations. These five social domains activate the same threat and reward responses in our brain that we rely on for physical survival.

---

[16]. http://davidrock.net/about/

Status is about relative importance to others. Certainty concerns being able to predict the future. Autonomy provides a sense of control over events. Relatedness is a sense of safety with others, of friend rather than foe. And fairness is a perception of fair exchanges between people.

The SCARF concept if applied can prove to be a boon to improve team collaboration at the workplace. Perceived threats and rewards can influence our behavior in different ways. If these threats and rewards can be managed to create a positive impact, it leads to an engaged and self-organized team.

Certainty and autonomy are directly related to the individual. For example, do you feel empowered in your team? Status, relatedness and fairness are factors of others' influence. For example, do you feel you have a strong bonding with your team and you enjoy working with them?

SCARF can be used in retrospectives to understand how the surrounding environment influences the five SCARF domains. If you can create an environment that creates a positive impact where individuals do not feel threatened then the transition time from forming to performing team development will drastically go down.

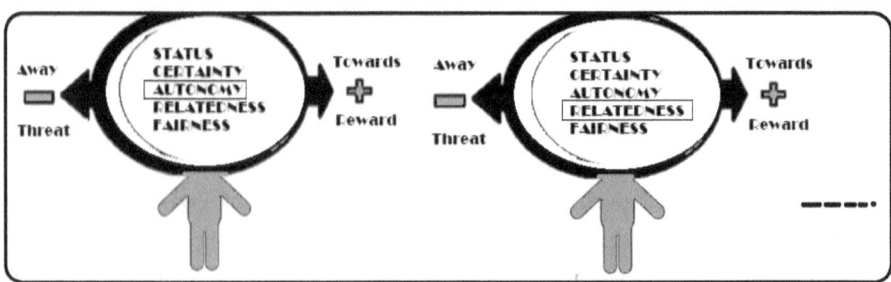

Instructions

- Explain the SCARF model and how it supports the team's self-organizing capabilities

- Start with the leadership. Discuss the five SCARF domains and ask them to think if the surrounding environment and their behavior is triggering a threat response or vice versa. Note the activities that are triggering a reward on the right side and the ones leading to a threat on the left side of each of the SCARF domains as indicated in the picture above

- For activities that are threat-focused, ask the leadership to come up with alternatives that would help decrease the threat factor and turn it into a reward. This helps them reflect on how the present environment is set up and what changes are required for maximizing rewards and minimizing threats

- Once the management comes up with their own data points, this exercise can be repeated with the teams. Ask them how they feel working with their leaders and how safe do they feel to experiment and make mistakes. The results can be compared to learn how management and the team perceive the same situation, and this could lead to the discovery of many thought-provoking findings

When this exercise was done with one of the teams, many interesting insights were uncovered. Communicating the vision and business strategies aid in providing certainty. Giving space to employees to offer feedback, giving them opportunities to learn, and recognizing their work contributes to the status factor. Providing transparency and establishing team norms promotes fair working relationships.

***

5. ROUNDTABLE

Situation: Keeping the format of the retrospective open and asking team members about their thoughts sometimes works well as it encourages team members to start expressing without any barriers.

Once, I met a couple of my close friends after a long time. We were very closely knit and shared everything with each other. Our relationship was perfect. However, I sensed a certain negative energy that particular day which I could not place. So, I tried to create a safe space for my friends to share what was going on. Sensing my openness, one of them immediately opened up to express some problems she was facing for which she felt there was nobody to help her out.

This situation could extend to teams as well. While things might be going smoothly, there could be certain underlying issues which might still need a resolution. Sometimes leaving the option open to members of the team and asking them what they want to talk about could trigger a good discussion.

Try asking your team members explicitly whether they have certain points to discuss and facilitate that conversation.

Instructions

- Make the team members sit in a position which indicates openness – a circle is a good idea
- Keep the environment casual and ask the team members to share any point they would like to bring up
- Note down the points on the board and facilitate a conversation about it. If certain issues need to be resolved, use any of the retrospective techniques to get to the root of the problem

* * *

6. DREAM CATCHER

Situation: As kids we all loved drawing analogies out of our dream. This works with teams too.

While I was shopping one day, my children bought a dream catcher and hung it in their bedroom. When I asked what the significance of dream catcher was, they told me that dream catcher was traditionally used as a talisman to protect sleeping people, usually children, from bad dreams and nightmares. Good dreams pass through and gently slide down the feathers to comfort the sleeper below. Bad dreams, however, are caught up in its protective net and destroyed, burned up in the light of the day.

After a few days of buying the dream catcher, I just started with a new team and I was doing a team building activity for them. The dream catcher concept came to my mind. I drew a dream catcher on the board, and described the significance of how it comforts people by preventing bad dreams. I asked members of the team to imagine how they would want to see their team to be like and what values it should have. I asked them to put up feathers for each of these values. I asked what qualities they would never like to have in their team and put them inside the net. Then we discussed ways to imbibe the good values in the team.

I also asked the team to think about precautions that can be taken so that the influence of unwanted traits captured by the net can be reduced. The team added many feathers like oneness, courage, respect, honesty and spotlight as values they wanted to have. The team added items like attitude, silo thinking, egoism, lack of commitment and trust inside the net. In this way, dream catcher can be used for a team discussion to envisage their "dream team". What characteristics they would like to have, the values they would like to possess and what are the traits they should not possess that hinder them from becoming a great team.

Another day I saw a team debating about their product and the features that can help improve its market value and what sort of features can cause more harm than benefit. I felt this discussion was very similar to the dream catcher analogy where the feathers represent the features that will benefit the product and add value. While the net represents the features that should not be added to the product and bad features that are detrimental to the product. Bigger feathers can be created to represent complex features that are more important and the net of the dream catcher represents bad dreams i.e. what customers do not want in the product.

Instructions

> - Draw the picture of the dream catcher picture or print the above image and give it the team name
> - Ask the team to imagine it as their dream team
> - Add feathers to represent good characteristics of their team
> - Add net to represent bad ones
> - Discuss how to enhance good characteristics and overcome the bad ones

* * *

7. BALANCED SANDBOX

Situation: If you are looking at ways to build a motivated team, then this technique will be of interest to you! This approach could be used for thinking about ways to promote intrinsic motivators and to build a healthy team culture.

All of us know the Dan Pink drive motivation theory that states Autonomy, Mastery and Purpose as the key factors for intrinsic motivation.

Autonomy is the ability to control your acts and make your decisions. In a team motivation can be fostered by letting team members work on their own goals that they are passionate about alongside the regular work, or trying to align organization work with their personal interests and passion. Mastery lets you foresee your potential and work to the fullest potential. Purpose talks about the "why" part i.e envisaging the bigger picture i.e vision or goal behind any endeavor.

So, on a team, if these three drivers are fostered then teams can be motivated intrinsically and it may lead to a team that has a drive for passion and excellence.

Draw the below picture on the board

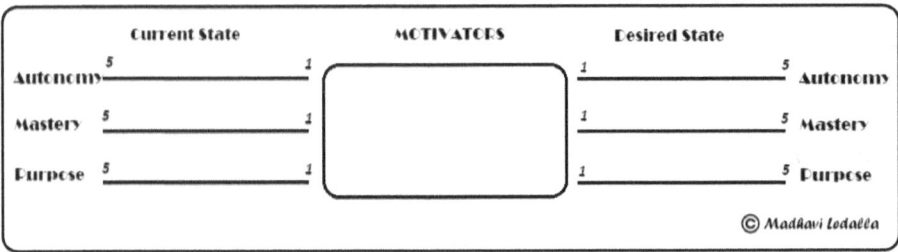

- Ask leadership to think the current levels of intrinsic motivators in the teams and note them on the left side of the picture
- Discuss the desired levels they would like to see their teams at and put them on the right side
- Ask them to think of ways to promote these key factors and note down ideas for reaching a maxima for each of these traits in the motivators section.

Repeat this exercise with teams

> Ask them to rate what are their intrinsic motivator levels on the team

> Think of avenues that can help them achieve greater scales

> Share the notes with leaders and this may lead to interesting insights around how teams and leadership perceive the motivation levels

It is a known fact that there needs to be a balance between the intrinsic and extrinsic motivators on any team for long-term sustainability. In order to discuss this balance, you can extend this exercise as detailed below.

An extension to this exercise is to think how to create a balanced sandbox for the teams so that they are motivated intrinsically and extrinsically.

Draw the picture below. List the intrinsic and extrinsic motivators and then discuss if there is a balance across both the types and what can be done to foster a healthy balanced sandbox for teams to experience happiness and joy.

PART NINE

Adding Layers to Retrospectives

CHAPTER 12

ADDING LAYERS TO RETROSPECTIVES

In this section additional constructs for beyond a single team and ways to use a combination of techniques are discussed.

- Daily retrospectives
- Cross-team retrospectives
- Distributed retrospectives
- Release retrospectives
- Leveraging Online Collaboration Tools
- Using a combination of collaboration frameworks
- Using same technique in different contexts

* * *

1. DAILY RETROSPECTIVES

While a retrospective is a formal platform for the team to reflect at the end of the sprint, nothing really stops the team from reflecting daily on how they are working together! If you are inquisitive about the benefits of a daily reflection, you will find this section interesting.

Daily reflection helps when the team is newly formed and they need to collaborate every day to be on the same page. As the team matures, I believe a fixed time reminder for daily reflection is not really needed. However, the team can decide if they wish to get into a continuous reflection mode every day at a prescribed time. Leave the choice to the team about how frequently they want to reflect - daily, weekly or fortnightly.

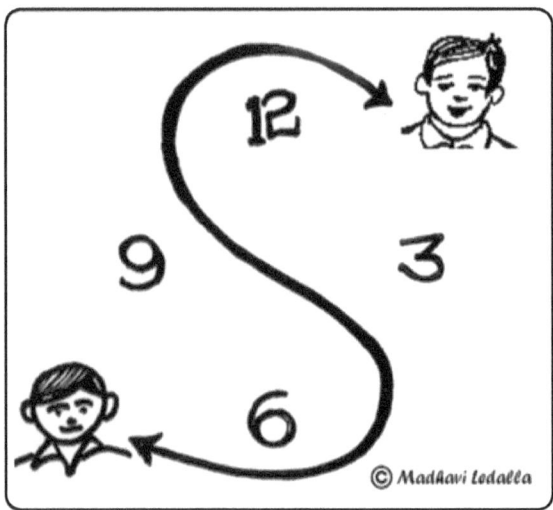

Daily retrospectives require a different process for facilitation as the time boxing has to be perfect and the outcome has to be valuable for sustainability.

While you can come up with your own variation for establishing a routine for the daily retrospective, here are a few one-minute toolkits to get you started.

- Each team member shouts out how their day was before leaving for the day
- Each team member shouts out what is the plan for the next day

- The team picks a yoga routine and while doing so they discuss how their day was, and what stopped them from moving ahead
- Each team member can put a star ranging from one star to five stars and comment if their stars are less than three and why
- Each member of the team describes their day in two or three words
- Each team member puts an appropriate smiley to indicate how their day was
- Each team member starts the day with a check-in protocol and leaves the day with a check-out protocol

* * *

2. CROSS-TEAM RETROSPECTIVES

Retrospectives are generally held at the end of each sprint, when the team gathers to look at the way they are working and identifies some commonly agreed-upon modifications, and improvements for the next sprint (or project).

There is a challenge in team-level retrospectives when the team is part of a big group of teams, involving complex and interdependent work of large scale. If teams perform retrospectives at their team level, there is a good chance that their focus is on short-term issues that are most concerning them alone.

The teams that perform retrospectives only at their team level, focusing on individual cycles, tend to be more focused on team-level decisions rather than aligning to the organization's long-term strategic goals and decisions as cited by Jutta Eckstein[17] in the book – *Agile Software Development in the Large*. Thus, effective coordination and communication among different teams is essential for organizations working on complex and interdependent functionalities. Cross-team retrospectives might be of help in such cases.

---

[17] https://www.amazon.com/Agile-Software-Development-Large-Diving/dp/0932633579

Purpose

The idea of holding a cross-team retrospective is to discuss common issues, critical impediments and achievements so that teams can benefit from each other's' journeys. This is not the space to discuss every small item that we usually discuss at team-level retrospective. Teams need to think through topics they would like to discuss in these sessions - topics that could be beneficial for other teams to know about.

Some teams I know conduct individual retrospectives and hold a dot-vote to decide on the topics that they want to discuss in the cross-team retrospective.

Discussion points

Here are some points that could be discussed, there could be others too:

- What works well for the teams, what is not working well and what they could improve?
- What we can do independently and what we cannot do independently?
- What did we try that was new and what do we want to try?
- What were the team's major achievements during this sprint and how did the team achieve them?
- What went wrong during the sprint and how do we plan to correct it?
- What were the most critical impediments and how did we resolve them?
- What have we learned?
- What still bothers us?
- What can we do differently?

The format of a cross-team retrospective is similar to a team level retrospective, but the focus should be on joint issues that were identified and additionally whatever might come up during the meeting. Generally, this retrospective is held after each team has conducted its own retrospective. However, few teams also alternate between a cross-team and individual team retrospectives.

Execution

You could hold the cross-team retrospective in one of two ways:

- **Variant 1:** Individual teams hold their own retrospectives. Then they can come together in a cross-team retrospective to discuss common issues, where each team sends a representative to this meeting
- **Variant 2:** Individual teams have their own retrospectives. Then all team members could attend the cross-team retrospective (rather than just sending a representative from each team)

It is helpful to use a visual aid during the retrospective, as visual radiators generate clear thoughts and you could cover all aspects. Here you see the picture of a format that covers a few common topics. It could be customized by changing the quadrants. Such a visual radiator may help the group to have fruitful discussions about facts that could have been missed in the individual team-level sessions.

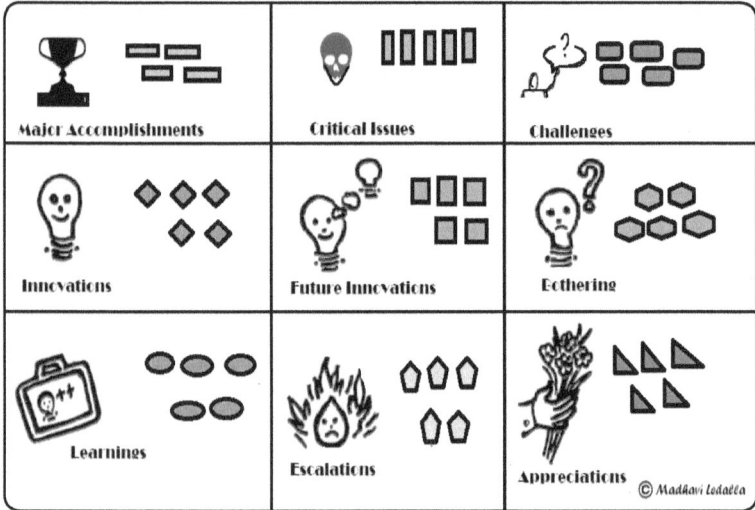

Frequency

Cross-team retrospectives should not become overkill for teams. Holding a cross-team retrospective following a team retrospective every time could be overwhelming. Teams could decide on the frequency based on the number of common issues they see, and they can always inspect and adapt to check how often they should hold such meetings.

Frequency depends solely on the need. Some teams have them after every third or fifth sprint or after achieving some milestones. However, if the teams are newly formed, you could have them more often, until they become stable.

Location

- If the teams are located together, you can hold these meetings in a conference room to enable face-to-face communication
- If the teams are spread out, you could use online collaboration tools so that teams can see each other

However, the former option is always best!

Benefits

- Visibility into systemic level issues and opportunities
- Faster resolution of organizational issues by harnessing collective experience and knowledge
- Opportunities for global optimization as inter team challenges get visibility
- Inter-team communication and collaboration capabilities improve
- Transparency between teams
- Sharing of best practices with other teams
- Collective brainstorming on challenges and impediments
- Learning from others challenges and successes instead of reinventing the wheel
- Brings to the forefront and resolving dependencies across the teams
- Engaged and motivated teams that ultimately lead to improved productivity levels

Make them effective

A retrospective on the cross-team retrospectives can be done once in a while to assess their effectiveness. Depending on the findings, the frequency and mode of conducting the retrospective could be modified.

Challenges

- A good facilitator is imperative to facilitate discussions in the right direction. Otherwise the meeting could descend into chaos
- Setting up a cadence for cross-team retrospectives could be a challenge if the teams are following different sprint schedules
- Time boxing the sessions could be tough

* * *

3. DISTRIBUTED RETROSPECTIVES

Retrospectives play a vital role for distributed teams as much as they do for co-located ones. However, when teams are distributed across various geographical locations, the facilitation becomes challenging. The distributed nature of teams adds another layer to the regular challenges of making the retrospective effective.

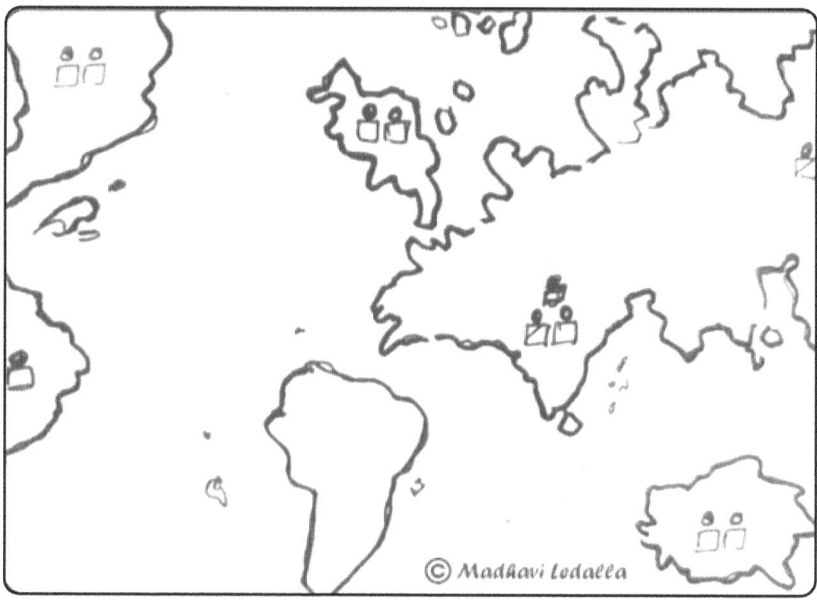

The biggest challenge that a geographically dispersed team faces is to find a way to leverage the essence behind these agile values "Individuals and interactions over processes and tools" and "The most efficient and effective method of conveying information to and within a development team is face-to-face communication."

The distributed team retrospectives pretty much go through the five stages of any general retrospective course, however listed below are some additional constructs that may help in planning and execution considering the distributed nature of the teams.

Preparation for the retrospective

- Engage a facilitator at every location to ensure streamlined and coordinated communication
- The facilitators at all locations should meet ahead of the team and finalize the agenda, and techniques to be used
- Decide which online tool will be used. It could also be a shared Word document or an Excel sheet that is accessible to all
- The facilitators should check the functioning of the tool and troubleshoot any network issues to save time during the actual retrospective. Have a dry run before the actual meeting
- Publish the agenda in advance so that all teams are ready
- Decide in advance the technique that will be used for holding the retrospective
- Facilitators should ensure that the team comes prepared with data for the retrospective

Create a working agreement

Come up with a working agreement for holding the retrospective. Your working agreement could cover the following points:

- Each site facilitator should lead the session
- At the beginning of every session, review any pending action items from previous retrospective and discuss the plan of action if they are important for follow-up
- Raise a hand or a yellow card in case someone feels the discussion is going off track
- Time box the discussion so that everyone gets a considerable amount of time to speak
- Make sure the discussions are interactive and open
- Facilitators should make note of the important points that come up
- Facilitators must take inputs from their respective sites and perform a quick retrospective about the distributed retrospective session
- Use a consensus technique such as fist-to-five or green cards to arrive at an agreement so that each site agrees to any decision made
- Take planned time-boxed breaks as needed

Process:

1. Set the stage

- The facilitators at the different sites should initiate the discussion
- Briefly go through the agenda
- Reiterate the prime directive[18]
- Get consensus on the working agreement
- Describe the technique

[18.] Norm Kerth, Project Retrospectives

2. **Initiate the retrospective**

    ➤ Hold a quick recap of the previous sprint retrospective to check if there are any pending items or items to carry forward

    ➤ One of the site facilitators puts down the technique to be used for the retrospective on the online collaboration tool

    ➤ Each site team member specifies their views on the collaboration tool.

    ➤ Facilitators could show a visual indicator, such as a "done" flag, once each site is finished

    ➤ At each site, the facilitator can go over their items and discuss, and give time to the other sites to give their comments, if any

    ➤ Repeat this round at all the sites

    ➤ Once all sites are done, do a quick check to see whether any site has any other comments

3. **Action plan**

    ➤ Each site could come up with action items and share with the other sites and take their views

    ➤ Repeat this round at all sites

    ➤ Once all sites are done, do a quick check to see whether any site has any other comments

    ➤ Consolidate the action plan and get a quick consensus

4. **Closure**

    ➤ Share the retrospective techniques, the data gathered and action plan with all sites

    ➤ Spend five minutes to get quick feedback across all sites on the retrospective event

    ➤ Facilitators at the various sites follow up and coordinate on the action plan

* * *

4. RELEASE RETROSPECTIVES

For any organization that has large-sized and complex projects with resources located at various geographical locations, a lot of interdependencies are inherent and a lot of coordination is required. People involved in running these types of projects need to constantly review and monitor their progress and delivery.

To effectively monitor and to continuously improve, different organizations adopt different mechanisms and methods at various stages in the lifecycle of the projects. Conducting release retrospectives is one such tool that has been effectively used to yield good results.

Before talking about release retrospectives, let us understand what a release is.

A release would typically last three to six months, sometimes even a year, depending on the organization's release cycle. A release comprises many sprints and the time box of each sprint could be two to four weeks.

Difference between a release retrospective and a regular retrospective

A regular retrospective provides an opportunity to inspect and adapt the sprint cycle to look back at how the sprint was and discuss ways to make improvements in the upcoming sprints.

A release retrospective is an opportunity to inspect and adapt the release cycle rather than the sprint cycle. Of course, the inspection points would vary when it comes to the release. The basic idea of doing a release retrospective is to review and evaluate an entire release, which spans through multiple sprints, for getting a high-level picture by involving all important stakeholders and the management team.

It is important for senior management, i.e., the product managers, development managers and product owners, and all other senior level stakeholders to be involved in the release and strategic planning to participate in a release retrospective. Since release retrospectives have a larger participation facilitation plays an extremely important role.

Frequency and duration of the release retrospective

A release retrospective is held at the end of the release and before starting the next release cycle. A schedule is worked out well in advance, and the date and time are communicated to all concerned stakeholders so that they come prepared with points of discussion.

Focus of a release retrospective

The focus of a release retrospective is to review how the release was with respect to strategic objectives, product quality emerging trends and other organizational goals.

Some of the common inspection points for a release retrospective could be-

- Current status of projects w.r.t strategic initiatives
- Organizational initiatives and the progress
- Organizational level key performance indicators
- Product quality
- Number of escaped defects
- Planned features versus delivered features
- Whether the features delivered were in the order of priority
- The number of features developed that were accepted
- The number of accepted features
- The number of issues reported by the customer and the length of time taken to fix those issues
- Whether the release date was extended, and if so, why
- Whether all the scope planned for the release were delivered
- The number of defects getting generated on previous enhancements

> Whether interim customer feedback is being taken
> New technology initiatives
> Infrastructure issues causing release delays
> Performance improvement initiatives
> Any new tools to be introduced
> The optimization that can be done at various levels
> Any effective strategies that were helpful

Of course, there could be many more such points. So, keep an open mind and note down pointers as they come up during your sprint.

The content discussed during the release retrospective can be categorized for better visualization. I would recommend classifying them into technology, development, process and quality groups.

This suggested grouping would best suit IT projects, so based on the nature of work, product or organization, you can design custom categories.

TECHNOLOGY	Technology Vision
	Current technological trends in market
	Business need to upgrade current to a new technology
DEVELOPMENT	# Number of features planned
	# Number of features developed
QUALITY	# Number of across different environments
	# Number of build breakages
	% Automation coverage
PROCESS	What is working well
	What are the challenges with the current process

© Madhavi Ledalla

Gathering Data

Here are few methods to gather customer feedback to discuss during the release retrospective.

- Regular customer meet-ups: Senior management could travel to the customers' location to get their feedback
- The point of contact or senior management could establish regular checkpoints with customers to collect their feedback
- You can conduct customer surveys with predefined questions and gather data via responses
- Periodic measurements to collect supporting data for key initiatives like Net Promotor Score

Preparation for the release retrospective

Usually, as the working agreement of what needs to be discussed in the release retrospective is formulated well in advance, the concerned people have enough time to come prepared with project data. The preparation time could be considerable depending on the inspection points chosen for discussion in the release retrospective.

Format

A release retrospective often spans across one or two days depending on the size of the project, the agenda and the number of teams involved. In some organizations, senior management and executive leadership participate, and the focus would be specific strategic objectives and goals.

Outlined below are few steps for facilitating a release retrospective. Discuss these with the team including senior management to know what everyone has to anticipate in preparation for the release retrospective.

- Make it clear that the objective of the release retrospective is to inspect and adapt the release cycle
- Reiterate the prime directive: Regardless of what we discover, the team truly understands and believes that everyone did the best job they could, given what they knew at the time, their skills, their abilities, the resources available and the situation on hand

- Review the strategic objective of the release so that everyone is aware of release goals and expected outcomes, the major events and release level metrics
- Discuss the release cycle timeline and the categories the release data can be grouped into
- Use any of the facilitation techniques, usually a timeline format is used for gathering the release data. Use affinity maps and grouping as needed to organize the data into different categories for better visualization to ease the discussions.
- Discuss the release using the quantitative and qualitative data gathered. Identify what worked well and what didn't
- For items that did not go well or for items that require improvement, brainstorm the probable causes and ways to improve the future work. Basis the discussions, formulate a plan for new initiatives at the organizational level that everyone agrees to implement. Procuring new tools, introducing new technology, process-related changes, new technical initiatives and new strategies could be a few examples
- Identify previous release retrospective action items and analyze if any of them still require any further action
- Come up with an action plan for the new goals identified in the current release retrospective

Every organization could have its own specific agenda/structure, based on the nature of the work; however, you could use a simple agenda for holding the release retrospective, as shown here:

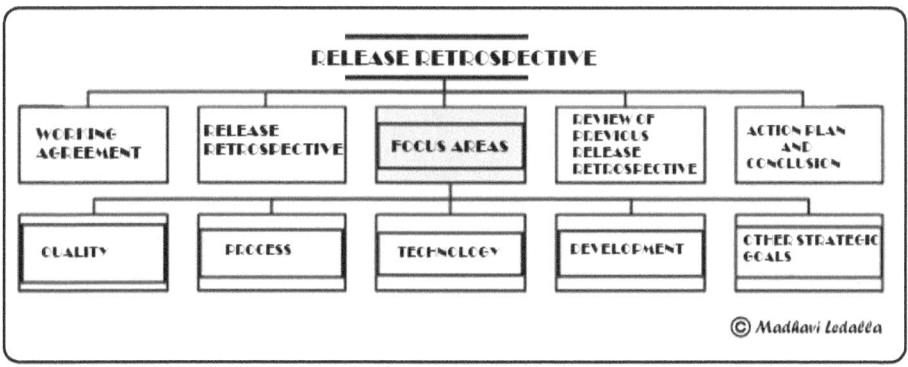

Benefits

- Focus on the strategic objectives and organizational level initiatives
- Review the health of the release
- Evaluate the release with regard to the key focus areas and come up with a strategy for the next release
- Review the lessons learned from the release cycle and discuss opportunities of improvement for the next cycle

Note: Some teams do a release retrospective in which all the teams and team members are involved. Norman Kerth's book 'Project Retrospectives' talks about a few techniques for running a large-scale retrospective in which many people are involved.

※ ※ ※

5. LEVERAGING ONLINE COLLABORATION TOOLS

I personally had a hard time doing retrospectives for distributed teams. The biggest challenge for geographically dispersed teams is finding ways to leverage the essence of "individuals and interactions over processes and tools", and the value behind the principle, "The most efficient and effective method of conveying information to and within a development team is face-to-face communication." However, by using some good collaboration tools, we can reap the benefits of face-to-face communication to some extent so that the retrospective can be effective!

One resource that has been helpful in this endeavor is Weave TM Platform[19] that was created by Luke Hohmann, Founder and CEO of Conteneo Inc., who has been my mentor in the virtual collaboration space. This platform features many collaboration frameworks that can be used with distributed teams, like Sail Boat, Plus/Delta and Learning Matrix. I published a few of my techniques on this website, so that they could be used in a distributed setup.

In my experience, Weave platform offers a lean forum for virtual collaboration. What I appreciate most about Weave™ platform is that all the retrospective game data - including the players' names - is collated into an Excel spreadsheet with a click of a button. The retrospective data can further be analyzed to check for any patterns, outliers and surprises.

There are other platforms like Retrium[20], Idea Boards, Trello or Google docs that can be used for online collaboration.

* * *

---

[19]. https://conteneo.co/
[20]. https://www.retrium.com/

6. USING A COMBINATION OF COLLABORATION FRAMEWORKS

Scenarios that require in-depth analysis and multiple layers of brainstorming can be tackled through a combination of frameworks. This approach requires breaking down the bigger issue into multiple smaller problems, prioritizing these smaller problems and mapping out how they are related to each other. The examples cited in this section will detail this method.

1. **Building a new product for a customer:** This will require the customer and the team to discuss several aspects and go through multiple sprints. So, the nature of the discussions must be manifold. Now, let us see how to use a combination of frameworks to address this situation.

    ➤ **Climbing a mountain:** This exercise can be used to discuss specific product requests to understand their needs. Visualize climbing the mountain as the goal of the product and the customer pain points as impediments to the trek. Ask customers to think how fast they can climb the mountain, i.e., how fast they want to build their product. Discuss enablers, i.e., what they want to see in their product. So, the outcome would be the final pain points and customer requests.

    ➤ **Dream catcher:** Now that we have captured the pain points and enablers, let us capture features that can be built to tackle the pain areas and leverage the enablers. Use dream catcher to come up with features that will help resolve the pain areas. The dream catcher itself represents customer requests and the new features can be represented by the feathers of the dream catcher. Use long feathers to represent bigger features that carry a complexity.

- **Product eel**: Now that you have identified the needs, use product eel for prioritization. Identify the critical features that must be built into the first release to address the customer pain points.

- **Mushroom cloud**: Break down the features using the "mushroom cloud" into smaller increments.

2. **Empathizing with customers:** You could use the below three techniques in sequence to empathize with your customers and build what they envisage in their product.

    - **The three monkeys:** If your team is working on a new product, then initially you could use the "the three monkeys" exercise to identify what the customer wants to see, hear and talk about their product

    - **Mushroom cloud:** Once you capture the ideas, use these ideas to brainstorm features that you would like to build using the "mushroom cloud"

    - **Time travel:** Then take these features and use "time travel" to prioritize

3. **Enhancing the existing product:** Suppose your product is already in the market, but the time has arrived to build additions. Let us see how to use a combination of collaboration frameworks to address this.

    - **Journey:** Start with the "journey" framework to discuss the product's journey in the past year, and visualize new ideas and features to add. Discuss impediments and the enablers in the product journey so far from different perspectives that include sales, marketing, users and customers

    - **Foresee the future:** Use this framework to discuss the updates, new enhancements that can be incorporated into the product to accommodate the new requests. Focus is to enhance customer gains and reduce the pain points as described by customers as revealed by the "journey" framework

- **Time travel:** Use this framework to prioritize the list for adding minimal marketable features in the different time horizons

4. **Surviving the competition:** In case your product is already half built, and you see competition coming up, let us see which techniques may work here:

    - **Candle light:** Start with "candle light" to discuss detractors and promoters, and what can be done to increase promoters and decrease detractors

    - **Set me free:** After capturing those ideas, use "set me free" to discuss any constraints the team oversees that would restrict them from implementing these ideas

5. **Team Collaboration:** Get away from products for a bit and see how a combination could be used to address an issue concerning a team as a whole.

    - **Shoot the ball:** Use this technique to allow the team to think on how they are working now and what they can do differently so that they can work as a real team, and not a working group

    - **Fly high:** Use "fly high" to identify what is in their control and what isn't for the team to work as a real team as envisioned in the previous step

* * *

7. USING THE SAME TECHNIQUE IN DIFFERENT CONTEXTS

The techniques that are discussed in the book are not rigid in the way they have to be applied. You can use them as guidelines and build your own interpretation, and use it for different contexts that best suit your team. Here are a few examples of how the same technique could be used in a different context with slight modifications to the structure:

- **Good to great:** Use this technique for an individual to reflect on her or his current state and what is the "best" version that she or he could get to, and the plan towards that version
- **Tasty cake**: Use this technique for personal reflection to think about individual goals and reflect on the work that one is doing that is not adding any value to one's life
- **Set me free:** Use this for yourself to think of the constraints that are refraining you from meeting your targets or goals
- **Foresee the future**: Use this for your team or for yourself to visualize where you or your team wants to be in the future
- **Make a wish**: Wish for the top three things your team would like to see in their team so that they become the happiest team
- **Candle light**: Envision the detractors and promoters for your team that would enable them to meet their team goals
- **Shoot the ball**: Use this technique to brainstorm what your delivery pipeline looks like currently, how you would like it to be in the next year and what measures you must take to get to the desired state
- **Pulse check**: Use this technique to check the pulse of the team or an individual team member
- **Fly high**: Identify what is in your control and what isn't in a team, and at an individual level to reach your targets
- **Dream catcher**: Debate the team aspirations or product aspirations from a stakeholder perspective

➢ **The three monkeys**: If your team is working on a new product, then initially you could use the "the three monkeys" exercise to identify what the customer wants to see, hear and talk about their product

➢ **Climbing a mountain (goal setting)**: If you want to break away from the traditional method of performance goal setting and looking for an unconventional way to drive the performance goal setting process for yourself or for your team, "climbing a mountain" is a good exercise to help you. At the end of the session, save the results of the discussion and assess the goals you should set for yourself or your team, and how you could work on achieving them. This process has several steps as detailed:

- **Step a: Set your goals:** You could set as many goals as you would like. Based on the number of goals you have set for yourself; you would have those many goal posts. For each goal, discuss with your manager/mentor about risks or impediments that you foresee. Speak about the steps you need to take to overcome the impediments. Discuss what will help you meet the goals so that you can work on those aspects

- **Step b: Visualize your goals:** After your initial discussion, prioritize your goals using 'goals iceberg' collaboration framework. This framework helps visualize your goals based on short-term and long-term timelines

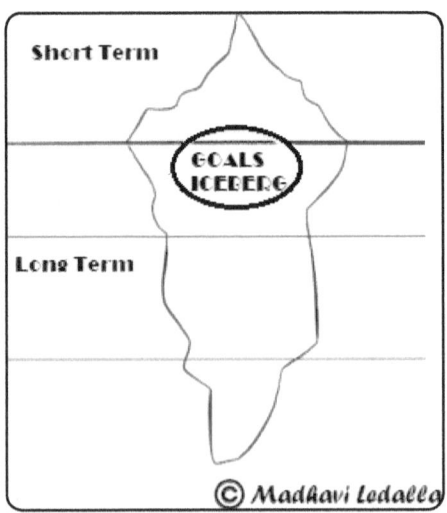

PART TEN

Tips and Tricks

TIPS AND TRICKS

CHAPTER **13**

This section talks about checklist for effective retrospectives and how one can measure the effectiveness of a retrospective, the maturity levels of a retrospective, and a simple survey for taking feedback after a retrospective. We also talk about describing the dysfunctions of a retrospective and finally the most important piece on how to embrace nature to naturally evolve new techniques.

- Effective Retrospectives Checklist
- Retrospectives Health Radar
- Retrospective Anti Patterns
- Retrospective Maturity Levels
- Retrospective Feedback
- Embrace the real world

* * *

1. EFFECTIVE RETROSPECTIVES CHECKLIST

Here is a checklist of items that you can consider to run a quick health check of the effectiveness of your retrospective. The checklist is categorized into sections to gauge how healthy and fruitful your retrospectives are.

For a good retrospective session, the responses for a few of these questions should be yes (the affirmative set) and for others it should be no (the negative set).

1. Facilitation

The affirmative set

- Does the facilitator iterate the prime directive to set the stage for the retrospective?
- Does the facilitator switch between different techniques at least once in five times?
- Does your facilitator use facilitation tools like white boarding and sticky notes?
- Does the facilitator ensure everyone in the team talks and shares their views?
- Do the retrospectives finish within the intended time box?
- Does the facilitator coach the team members on identifying the reason and possible solutions for issues being reported?

The negative set

- Does the facilitator have opinions about specific team members?
- Is the facilitator especially supportive to few specific members in the team?
- Do the retrospectives happen at the same place every time?

2. Team Involvement

The affirmative set

- Does the whole team participate in the retrospectives?
- Do team members openly share their views during the retrospectives?
- Are teams open and feel safe about sharing feedback?
- Are team members working on the retrospective action items?

The negative set

- Do team members have to be forced to come to the retrospectives?
- Are team members doing the sprint work during the retrospectives and speak occasionally?
- Do you see too much time is spent complaining or finger-pointing at each other?
- Are team members distracted and not fully present in the retrospective?

3. Effectiveness

The affirmative set

- Does the team refer to the previous sprint action items to ensure completeness?
- Are the retrospective action items time boxed and outcome focused, while ensuring assigned owners?

The negative set

- Do you see the same impediments coming up during retrospectives?
- Do the retrospectives become people specific and end up as a blame game?
- Do the retrospectives end up as complaining sessions without team members taking any ownership?

4. Closing

The affirmative set

- Do the retrospective action items resonate with the SMART[21] acronym and owned by specific people?
- Do the retrospectives end with a celebration?

The negative set

- Do the retrospectives end with discussions turning off topic without concluding on next steps?
- Do people feel threatened if similar problems are recurring in the retrospectives?
- Are all the artifacts created during the retrospectives trashed without saving them for future reference?
- Do team members leave the retrospective with a fear of repercussions for openly voicing their thoughts on the impediments?

* * *

---

[21]. https://en.wikipedia.org/wiki/SMART_criteria

2. RETROSPECTIVES HEALTH RADAR

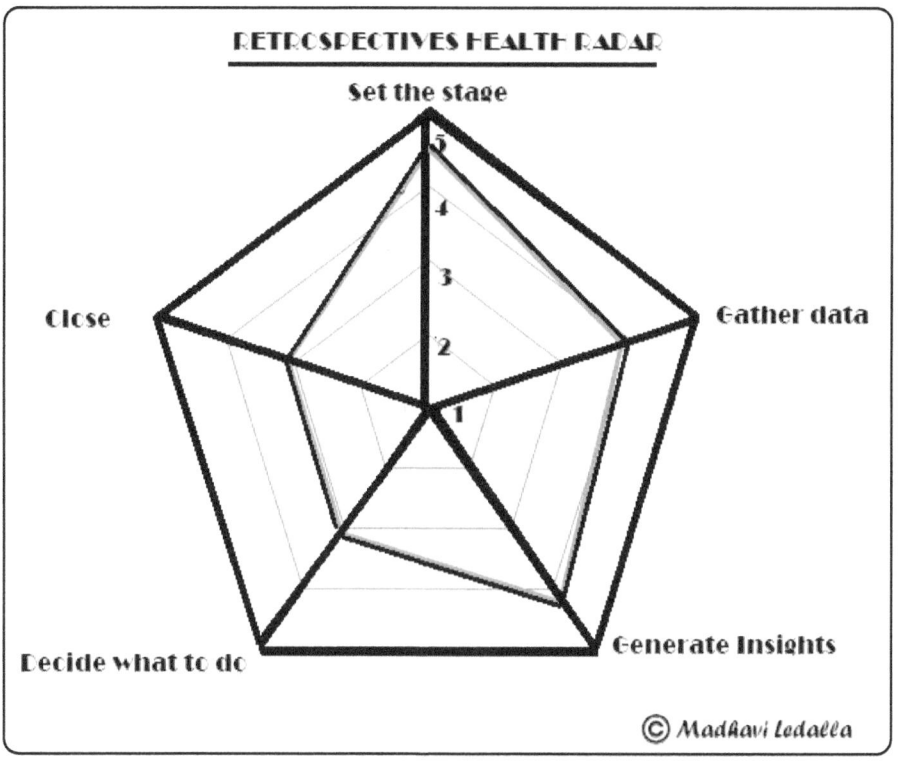

Use the following framework to check the effectiveness of the retrospective quantitatively. You can also use it to improve the effectiveness of the retrospectives. The framework is built around the standard retrospective stages explained by Esther Derby and Diana Larsen, in their book *'Agile Retrospectives'*.

SET THE STAGE		
(On a scale of 1-5, 5- most effective/always happens, 1- least effective/never happens)		
SNO	CHECKLIST ITEM	RATING
1	The facilitator ensures team is informed of the place and duration of the retrospective.	
2	The facilitator thanks the team for whatever they have done in the sprint.	
3	The purpose of retrospective is made clear to team members.	
4	The expectations of team are set right by iterating the retrospective prime directive.	
5	Team members' feedback is sought if they have any specific expectations from the retrospective.	
6	The facilitator discusses action items from the previous sprint to check for the completion status.	
7	Team members take time to acknowledge each others' accomplishments since the previous retrospective.	

GATHER DATA		
(On a scale of 1-5, 5- most effective/always happens, 1- least effective/never happens)		
SNO	CHECKLIST ITEM	RATING
1	The facilitator surprises the team by using new data gathering methods and challenges the team to think from a new perspective.	
2	The facilitator uses fun and engaging activities during the retrospective.	
3	Every team member voices their opinions.	
4	The team members are able to come up with data points for discussion within 5 to 10 minutes.	
5	The team is able to identify impediments and successes during the sprint.	
6	Quantitative data such as a team's quality metrics, productivity, predictability, cycle time is used for reflection and discussion along with other subjective information.	
7	The data gathered is grouped to identify trends that emerge.	
8	A clear trend emerges from the data - this means that one can visualize how the team thinks and feels based on the data.	
9	Visual radiators such as task board and burn down charts are used for discussions during the retrospective wherever appropriate.	

GENERATE INSIGHTS

(On a scale of 1-5, 5- most effective/always happens, 1- least effective/never happens)

SNO	CHECKLIST ITEM	RATING
1	Team members are asked the right questions that led to insights on the sprint.	
2	The team discusses ways to minimize impediments and maximize opportunities that helped them meet goals.	
3	The team identifies what really worked for them during the sprint and what did not.	
4	The team discusses risks they foresee for future sprints.	
5	The team is able to identify root causes for impediments.	
6	The team is able to identify reasons for pain and pleasure points during the sprint, and ponder on the gathered data.	

DECIDE WHAT TO DO

(On a scale of 1-5, 5- most effective/always happens, 1- least effective/never happens)

SNO	CHECKLIST ITEM	RATING
1	The data from insights is properly organized so that the team has a clear visibility on the happening of the previous sprint.	
2	Team develops actionable items based on insights generated to help them inspect and adapt.	
3	Team uses any method like the 80-20 rule to identify the action items to get the next sprint better.	
4	Action items are prioritized to arrive at the top 3-5 action items that the team wishes to work on in the next sprint.	
5	Team members volunteer and own the action items they have to complete.	

CLOSING

(On a scale of 1-5, 5- most effective/always happens, 1- least effective/never happens)

SNO	CHECKLIST ITEM	RATING
1	Team quickly discusses how the event was and anything they would like to change for the next retrospective.	
2	Team members thank others for having received help from them.	
3	Closing is followed by a small celebration.	

The health of the retrospective will be good when a few key ideas get implemented.

- Understand the purpose - to learn and not blame
- Do not experiment with too many new things
- Try plain vanilla first. Then add the toppings!
- Ask the team how they would like to do the retrospective, get their thoughts and buy-in.
- There is no single right answer for how to make the retrospectives effective - each team has its own flavor and liking. Find out from the team.
- Facilitate and drive it!

* * *

3. RETROSPECTIVE ANTI PATTERNS

The purpose of retrospectives is to get better with every sprint. However, when retrospectives are misused, it leads to some undesirable outcomes. If these outcomes are not handled well, then the essence of the retrospective is lost. As facilitators and team members, we need to be aware of these anti patterns so that we don't fall into dysfunctional traps. When the retrospective feedback is misrepresented, it leads to negative results. Let us explore a couple of retrospective anti patterns.

- **Yesterday's weather:** The team does not check the status on the action items that came up during the previous retrospective. They do not care if the items they discussed in the previous retrospective were implemented and if yes what the impact was

- **Blame Game:** If the environment is not set right, team members use retrospective feedback to blame each other and eventually it becomes a war room. Personal attacks lead to the team breaking down and working in silos. Individual team members start wondering, "What's in it for me?", and focus on their personal goals rather than team goals that leads to anti-collaboration

- **Output is used to measure individual performance**: When team members appreciate the fact that they could have done better, managers use this data against them in performance appraisals and hold individuals accountable for it. Here they focus on individuals rather than helping resolve root cause. This may lead to team members only discussing about positives, and refrain from talking about blockers and issues

- **Retrospectives are made public**: Retrospectives are recorded and made available to other teams by management without the teams' consent. Teams may feel unsafe to talk in such situations and the whole purpose of retrospectives is defeated

- **Local optimization**: Focus is only on team issues and issues that need attention at the organizational level are often ignored. The result is that the real root cause may never get addressed

- **Focus is on symptoms**: The problem is fixed superficially looking at the symptoms without a proper dissection of the root cause, and the result is that such items may keep coming up often again and again

- **Not outcome focused:** Many times, at the end of the retrospective, employees do not have any solid steps or a plan to work on action items. For example, if the retrospective action item is to "improve collaboration", what are the top three steps the team is agreeing upon that will enable the team to reach this outcome is not well thought out. Basically, there is no accountability on the part of team members for working on action items

- **Driven by facilitator's agenda**: This one especially holds good for the facilitator. Having a neutral mindset is important for a retrospective. As a facilitator if you go to a retrospective thinking that there is a specific reason behind an issue, and if the root cause or outcome is orthogonal to your thoughts, then you may tend to influence the team based on your thought process

- **Closed ended questions:** This is an important tip for the facilitators. Sometimes a facilitator is focused on coming up with answers and asks closed ended questions. This restricts the team from thinking and prevents them from reflecting on the available options and possibilities

- **Excluding few members:** Sometimes few team members miss retrospectives and if this is not raised as a concern it becomes a norm for people not to attend. Owing to this, the team loses the opportunity to get the perspective from those who are absent. You may miss out on some important points or ideas from those people. Similarly, those who are absent miss the context of the team health, and eventually if it becomes a practice, they may not get along with the team. Retrospective is a team game!

- **Lack of diversity**: If the same technique is used again and again, and run by the same facilitator, the engagement level of participants may begin to drop. Having the facilitator in the team member's role and team members in facilitator's space helps them get a perspective of each other's role and helps them empathize with each other

- **Students' syndrome**: Team postpones the retrospective thinking there is nothing for them to improve till the last responsible moment when they realize they missed the train all the while

- **Passive participation**: Not all team members are actively involved, they are present but do not participate and share their opinions. In this case we miss out on collective wisdom and lose the opportunity to improve as a team

- **Death by meeting**: Sometimes retrospectives begin and go on for hours at a stretch and lack a solid conclusion. This will eventually frustrate the team on numerous reasons and leads to other undesirable consequences, and the team may end up not coming to retrospectives if this syndrome continues

* * *

4. RETROSPECTIVE MATURITY LEVELS

For those who would like to check where the teams stand with respect to team maturity in internalizing the concept of retrospective as a heartbeat into their team rhythm, this section may provide some good ideas.

A maturity model for team retrospectives is presented here with the intent to provide a structure for assessing your team or organizational capabilities in doing these retrospectives and aid in planning a better strategy for devising improvements for existing processes.

This model is divided into six levels.

Maturity Level	Description	Criteria
Level -0	No retrospectives	Team does not do retrospectives
Level -1	Opinion-based retrospectives with no feedback loops.	Retrospectives are done, action items are implemented based on some hypothesis, but there is no check on whether the changes made helped/hindered the team.
Level-2	Opinion-based retrospectives with feedback loops.	Teams reflect on the outcomes and discuss the impact of the changes implemented.
Level-3	Data-driven retrospectives without feedback loops.	Retrospectives are backed by supporting quantitative data, but there is no reflection on whether the changes made helped/hindered the team.
Level-4	Data-driven retrospectives with feedback loops.	Retrospectives are backed by supporting quantitative data and this data is recorded and in fact used to assess the outcome and impact.
Level-5	Data-driven multi-team retrospectives.	Same as level 4 but happens in a multi-team context

* * *

5. RETROSPECTIVE FEEDBACK

Here is a sample template on how feedback can be taken from individual team members post the retrospective to assess its effectiveness.

1. Holistically, how valuable did you find the experience of participating in the retrospective and why?

1	2	3	4	5
Worthless	Somewhat useful	No Impact	Beneficial	Extremely Productive

2. Do you think you were able to voice your concerns openly?

1	2	3	4	5
Never	Seldom	Sometimes	Most of the time	Always

3. How safe did you feel to share your thoughts with others in the retrospectives?

1	2	3	4	5
Not at all	It depends on the participants	Sometimes	Most of the times	Always

4. Do you think your ideas are heard during the retrospectives?

1	2	3	4	5
Not at all	It depends on the participants	Sometimes	Most of the times	Always

5. On a scale of 1 to 10 how effective are your retrospectives now and why?

6. What do you need to go to the next level for improving your current retrospectives?

7. Given a magic wand, what is the one thing that you would add to the retrospectives?

8. Given a magic wand, what is the one thing that you would like to eliminate from your retrospectives?

9. Which part of the retrospective did you the enjoy most and why?

10. What makes you feel an accomplished person when you come out of the retrospectives? Do your current retrospectives resonate with this thought of yours?

* * *

6. EMBRACE THE REAL WORLD

Often, our everyday life brings us several interesting experiences that have the potential to be learning experience. It helps to take these experiences to the teams we work with and apply the learnings for improvement of current processes. Keep a close eye on the world around you, and see if there is any connection between your life and nature. See if you can relate to and connect real world and absorb the happenings with those in teams and organizations. When you can connect these, people can relate to them better. Instead of using imaginative stories for reflection, if you use real-world scenarios, you will be able to see a better engagement, as the connection happens organically.

The techniques cited are based on how I tried to relate real-world scenarios with team situations so that team members could relate, experience and think naturally so that ideas could emerge progressively.

A word of caution, success depends on how well the facilitator can link natural circumstances and create an environment so that teams get involved, and can embed themselves into the cited situation. We are not trying to force fit a scenario into a problem and trying to say that there is a tailor-made solution. We are just trying to experiment using natural situations that happen around us.

The core belief is that everyone is fully competent and resourceful, and every individual is capable of making sound decisions to solve her or his own problems. As a coach/facilitator one's effectiveness lies in bringing the best by provoking team members to see things from a different perspective. Usually teams/individuals think in their own black boxes that they draw for themselves. By using light weight structures i.e., a thinking container, you are trying to break these set boundaries and encouraging them to think outside of their normal beliefs. This may help them see from a new perspective that they haven't thought about so far.

Here is a basic template for any new person who would like to experiment or create her or his own ideas:

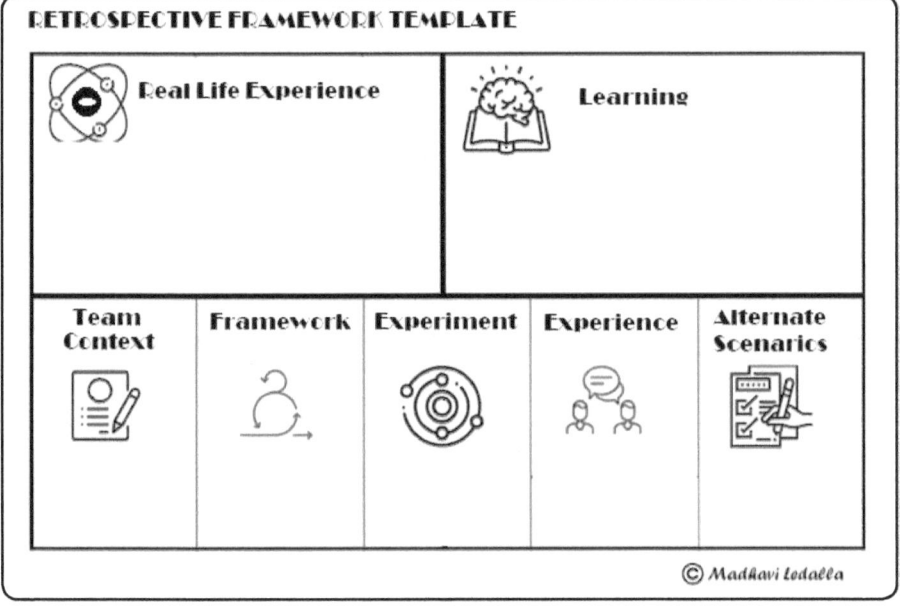

1. **Real-life experience**: Scenario observed from Nature around her or him

2. **Learning**: Reflect on this real-life experience and think if you can use it in your work situation

3. **Individual/Team context**: Is there any team or a personal situation that is similar to what you have observed in the scenario in step 1 and 2

4. **Framework**: Create a light weight structure using the metaphor for sharing the experience with the team or for a personal reflection.

5. **Experiment**: Use the framework/metaphor with the team to help brainstorm on the given situation

6. **Experience**: How did it work, capture this after you use the day-to-day life metaphor in your work situation.

7. **Alternate scenarios:** Think if there are other alternate scenarios where the same example can be used, apart from the instance listed in step 3

Example:

1. Real-life experience	Flying kite, kite getting stuck, how we removed, how tangles on ground were removed.
2. Learning	How did we resolve impediments in our control and those not in our control - i.e., tangles on the ground versus removing kite from electric wires?
3. Team context	Teams juggling between impediment they can resolve and for which they need support. They lack clarity on what they can do by themselves and what they cannot.
4. Framework	Create a "fly high" technique.
5. Experiment	Facilitate the discussion using the framework.
6. Experience	What went well and what did not go well when you applied the metaphor to the problem.
7. Alternate scenarios	Can be used for personal goal setting, to come up with a list of to-do things to meet your goals. Then separate the to-do things that you can act right away which are in your control, and others for which you need external help.

EPILOGUE

Retrospectives can be approached with an innovative mindset (thinking outside the box) by looking at the broader context of the challenge or the situation. Teams/individuals can bring their own imagination, knowledge and experiences to the table to create games for starting meaningful discussions. I personally saw visible improvements in productivity, quality, one-to-one coordination and collaboration after using some of the frameworks from this book.

The frameworks are meant to create a lightweight structure where you are creating a platform for teams to think beyond the normal boundaries and look for options.

- Observe the different situations the teams are dealing with and envisage the pattern of circumstances the team is going through
- Check if any of the frameworks presented in this book can be useful to deal with the situation
- If you cannot use these exercises as is, then make changes to customize to suit the needs of your team

The frameworks in this book are devised based on specific scenarios. As you would have figured out by now, these frameworks have been divided into logical clusters for better visualization. Try to associate the situation with your team and check if any of the frameworks can be related to. These frameworks may help you tackle different situations that you see in your team from a different perspective of solving a problem.

These exercises have emerged owing to what I have experimented and observed with my teams. I came up with frameworks that can help picture their state and thus can help connect to the team organically. One size does not fit all. You may get different results in your team. Hence, be open to experiment, learn and adapt the frameworks as per your need.

Try different exercises under the same cluster so that the teams are taken by surprise. The whole idea is to transform the environment for effective brainstorming and make teams get out of their comfort zones. This book will encourage you to come up with your own frameworks for problem solving.

The moral of the story is to use actual work and life experiences to innovate new ways of making the retrospectives fun and engaging, in addition to being educational and transformative. The intent of sharing games and techniques in this book is to help you, dear reader, get your adrenaline flowing so that you can come up with your own methods to create more effective retrospectives.

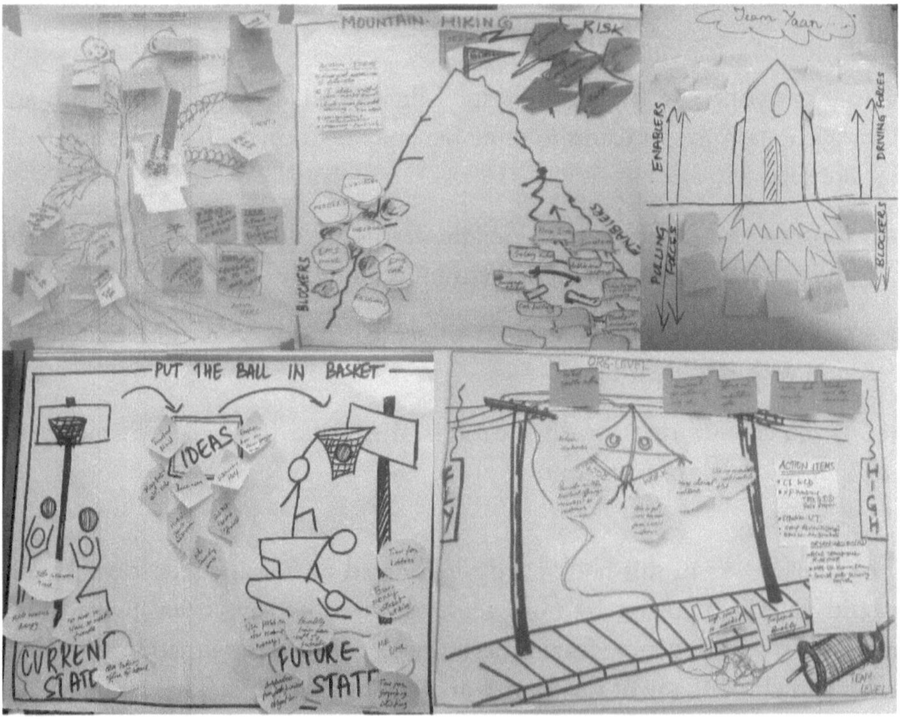

ABOUT THE AUTHOR

Madhavi Ledalla was born and raised in the city of Nawabs- Hyderabad. Her educational background involves a degree in Electronics and Communications Engineering and she also holds a post-graduation in Information technology.

Being a mother, she realized that learning is a two-way street. While her daughters were learning from her, she noticed that she was also learning from them. Everyday became a new experience and she realized that every space can be a learning space if we surrender to, 'I know it all' attitude. Also, being married to a doctor, she learnt how to feel one's pain and look for possibilities to help resolve the discomfort that one goes through, this helped her empathize with people. She drew from her experiences and it helped her look for creating the spaces in her work, that are described throughout the book.

She was introduced to Agile in the year 2008 and since then she has been working towards making the process more engaging and creative. She is a firm believer of the saying, "A picture is worth 1000 words". She loves to see everyone getting creative in solving a problem rather than conventional serious discussions. You will often hear her say, "Get creative to solve your problems".

Her deep passion for transforming the world of work has led her to be associated with transformational work with the organizations. Her expertise lies in coaching, to help people meet their professional and personal aspirations. She aims to create an environment where people can flourish and succeed. She is deeply passionate about building teams that are focused on outcomes instead of outputs.

She loves conducting customized workshops which include User Story, Product Owner, Scrum Master, Design Thinking, Release Planning and Portfolio Concepts that focus around improving teamwork and leadership capabilities. She has provided consulting support to several multinational and Indian companies. As a change management and agile consultant, she advised business leaders and teams.

Her professional portfolio includes training and coaching in varied agile methods including Scrum and Kanban, and other Scaling frameworks. She played multiple roles that include Scrum Master, Coach, Project Manager and Technologist during her career. Her niche consulting segments are: Leading transformation pilots to prepare a smooth path for the transformational change; Organizational assessments to assess the current state of an agile transformation; Setting up organizational portfolios and making work visible to set alignment across the organizations starting from the portfolio to teams; and Large distributed retrospectives using innovative games.

Madhavi is committed to serving the agile community by getting involved in various activities that include volunteering and organizing community events. She often participates and speaks at local as well as global events which gives her a platform to share her knowledge with a larger audience.

www.ingramcontent.com/pod-product-compliance
Lightning Source LLC
Chambersburg PA
CBHW020859180526
45163CB00007B/2556